CREATING HABITS FOR A FUNCTIONAL LIFE

Bishop R. S. Walker

CREATING HABITS FOR A FUNCTIONAL LIFE
By Bishop Rodney S. Walker, I

Copyright ©2006 by Bishop RS Walker Ministries formerly
Another Touch of Glory/Rodney S. Walker Ministries

Published by Bishop R.S. Walker Ministries formerly Another
Touch of Glory Press
2760 Crain Highway
Waldorf, Maryland 20601
Voice (301-843-9267) - (877-200-8967)
Fax (240-585-7093)
Web address: http://www.bishoprswalker.com
E-mail: admin@bishoprswalker.com

ISBN-13: 978-0692424070 (Bishop R S Walker Ministries)
ISBN-10: 0692424075
Published in the United States of America

Some scripture quotations taken from AMPLIFIED BIBLE,
Copyright@ 1954, 1958, 1962, 1964, 1965, 1987 by The
Lockman Foundation. All rights reserved. Used by permission.
(www.Lockman.org)

Some scripture quotations contained herein are from the New
Revised Standard Version of the Bible, copyright 1989, by the
Division of Christian Education of the National Council of
Churches of Christ in the U.S.A. Used by permission. All
rights reserved.

Dedication

This book is dedicated to my parents, Brozzie and Mary E. Walker. I want to take this opportunity to express my appreciation for my parents. They were and still are instrumental in my growth and development up to this point in my life. There are many instances of their parenting and guidance that I am able to associate with good, solid growth and developmental principles. I have learned so much from my father and mother. I realize that I was spared from developing many bad habits that could have led me to even more addictions and bondages than the ones I experienced. I learned great principles of patience, overcoming physical barriers, and staying on course in difficult times from my father and mother, and, in addition, I have learned from them how to push myself to accomplish particular things when I was uncertain about my ability to do so. My father taught me to be loyal, committed, and dependable, not just by what he said to me, but also from his great example. I can never repay them for all that they have given to me. I ask God's blessing over their lives as I continue to do the work of His ministry.

Foreword
by
Rev. Don DeGrate, ThD

I had the privilege and the pleasure of meeting Dr. Walker for the first time during a commencement exercise for a Bible college where we both were keynote speakers. Being very impressed with his message, I began to have fellowship with him and discovered that we had shared similar life experiences, especially in the ministry. In a follow-up telephone conversation I learned that he was writing a new book on a subject that could be applicable to anyone regardless of race, culture, age, religious denomination, social status, or even professional career. As we talked, he asked me to write the foreword for the book. Of course not having read the manuscript, I asked for a copy of it. After discovering the great information within its pages, I concluded that this book could be the very key to the deliverance of millions of people who are struggling with all types of strongholds and addictions if they apply the principles that the writer is sharing. As a pastor, I meet many people who deal with all kinds of issues that are addressed in this book, and I recommend it to be used in counsel as well as for personal reading. I thank Dr. Walker for such a needed source of life-changing information.

Foreword

by

Apostle Louis S. Greenup, Jr.

"And ye shall know the truth, and the truth shall make you free." (John 8:32, KJV)

In this book by Prophet Rodney Walker, you will come to understand the truth about how God's grace and power can deliver you from every bondage, habit, or addiction that has a stronghold on your life.

Are you tired of living in defeat? Do you want to fulfill your destiny and purpose in Christ? Are you burdened for your loved ones, friends, and associates who are bound by bad habits and addictions? Is there a stronghold that's hindering your walk with God?

This book will touch your life, whether you are male or female, young or old, married or single, chief apostle or layperson, sinner or saint. By following the roadmap that is provided, you will find yourself in a state of reflection, then on a journey of restoration, and ultimately in a place of revelation. Yes, it is through the power of the cross and the blood of the Lamb that we are redeemed, delivered, and set free from every demonic bondage and addiction. It's time for the shackles to be broken! We need to walk and live in the victory of our authority in Christ every day! Hallelujah!

Prophet Walker gives us profound wisdom on how

to rise up above the circumstances of life and challenges us to deal with our negative habits and addictions. We don't have to live in denial; we can defy the attacks of the Enemy through the power of prayer, worship, and the Word of God. Take heed when the Prophet says, "Deal with your addictive behavior! Come out of hiding!" " Admit it and quit it!" "You relinquish everything when there is a heartfelt surrender!" "We must deal with what is going on in our thought life!" "Anyone who is not preparing to win is already preparing to fail!" and, finally, "Meditate on the Word both day and night."

I encourage everyone who is ready to go to the next level in his or her life, relationships, and ministries to study this book. I believe you will receive the confidence and courage you need to confront, conquer, and control the negative habits and addictions that are trying to hinder or stagnate your future. Please take note, as the book shares, "Every decision that we make has either a promise or a penalty attached to it."

Decide today that the Word of God will have the preeminence in your life, and be in agreement with 2 Corinthians 5:17: "Therefore if any man be in Christ, he is a new creature: old things are past away; behold, all things are become new."(KJV)

You are free! You are delivered! Your bondages are broken! Your chains are loosed!

By applying the principles of this book, you will receive divine information for total transformation!

Appreciation

I thank Bishop Ralph L. Dennis, Jr. for the counsel and mentoring as he walked with me through some of my very difficult places that I personally experienced in times past that contributed to the knowledge I now have that has been inserted within the pages of this book. I thank Elder Tracy Morgan for the first editing of the book and the countless number of hours she put in to make this possible. All your work will never go unnoticed. Thank God also for my wife and children for releasing me to do this writing. Thank you again for a job well done.

CONTENTS

Should We Listen to a CD That Has One Gospel
Song on It?
Can We Listen to Regular Music and Still Serve
God?
What God Says About You
Death and Life are in the Power of the Tongue
Who is Mentoring You?

Jesus Stooped Down
The Choice Is Yours
Fill Your Mouth With the Word of God
How to Proclaim Victory

Present Your Body a Living Sacrifice
Are You Suffering From a Stronghold?
Gain Control of Your Mind
Do You Have Control Over Your Mind?

Chapter 1

Understanding Habits and Addictions

Where did all of our bondages and addictions originate? Cigarettes, drugs, and alcohol do not suddenly bind a person; addiction is a slow process that often starts in our childhood. It is of vital importance that we deal with the addictions in our lives. Not dealing with them will greatly affect our financial security and will cause a greater bondage.

Money magnifies what you are already doing. If you are prospering and have a drinking or drug problem, you will more than likely spend more on alcohol or drugs. But you can take steps to become strong enough to defeat the Enemy on every hand. God has favored us with His power and knowledge and has provided us with the power and ability to break every addiction and bondage.

Why do we need to talk about freedom from addictions? Romans 3:23 says, *"For all have sinned, and come short of the glory of God."*

This does not give us the license to sin! It means that we do not measure up to the sinless work of Jesus Christ. If you are around folks who are leading you deeper into bondage, get off the track now and go God's way. God wants you to have the best! Why is it necessary to stop doing things that are morally wrong? If all have sinned and come short of the glory of God, then why do we need to deal with issues regarding bondages and addictions? Because there is not one person who can truthfully say that he or she has not sinned! If we keep meditating on the fact that the Bible says all have sinned and come short of the glory of God, then I am persuaded that we won't do anything to better ourselves. So although it may be a sacrifice, you will have to turn from your wicked ways! If you are in a group that keeps leading you deeper into bondage, then leave and start going God's way so that He can favor you with His blessings. **God desires for you to have His absolute best!** He wants us to live in the best houses, drive the best cars, wear the best clothes, and be prosperous in every way. **However, He does not want us to have the best on the earth and go to hell!** He would rather that we have nothing and go to heaven rather than to have everything and go to hell. Therefore, deal with your addictions and bondages.

The Righteous vs. the Unrighteous

He that overcometh shall inherit all things, and I will be His God, and he shall be my son. But the fearful, and unbelieving, and the abominable, and murderers, and whoremongers, and sorcerers, and idolaters, and all liars, shall have their part in the lake which burneth with fire and brimstone: which is the second death. (Rev. 21:7-8)

In this scripture, God has put fear in the same categories as the unbelieving, the abominable, the murderer, the whoremongers, the sorcerers, the idolaters, and all liars. You can be straight in all seven areas, but if you are full of fear, then you stand a chance of burning in the lake of fire. Fear has to do with what is in your heart! You cannot "faith" and "fear" at the same time. The just shall live by **faith!** The scripture also includes **"all liars."** You may have at one time or another said, "I don't lie—I just don't tell the whole truth." A lie is a lie! It is either an absolute truth or an absolute **lie!** There are no categories of "little lies" and "big lies." God mentions several classes of people who are assured of burning in the lake of fire. For the believer, there is Sonship (rightful heir) and blessings with God forever. For the unrepentant person who is designated under the listed categories, there will not be bliss, but burning in the lake of fire, which is the second death.

Know ye not that the unrighteous shall not inherit the Kingdom of God? Be not deceived: neither fornicators, nor idolaters, nor adulterers, nor effeminate, nor abusers of themselves with mankind, nor thieves, nor covetous, nor drunkards, nor revilers, nor extortioners, shall inherit the kingdom of God. (1 Cor. 6:9-10)

All of us must live sanctified lives or we will not inherit the kingdom of God. So we must deal with the bondages and addictions in our lives. Do not push them under the carpet nor pretend that they do not exist. If you have no faith, deal with it; if you are unbelieving, deal with it; if you have fear in your life, deal with it; whatever the situation is, deal with it. **You** must raise your standards!

Know ye not that the unrighteous shall not inherit the kingdom of God? Be not deceived: neither fornicators, nor idolaters, nor adulterers, nor effeminate, nor abusers of themselves with mankind, nor thieves, nor covetous, nor drunkards, nor revilers, nor extortioners, shall inherit the kingdom of God. (1 Cor. 6:9-10 KJV)

Do you not know that the unrighteous and the wrongdoers will not inherit or have any share in the kingdom of God? Do not be deceived, (misled): neither the impure and immoral, nor idolaters, nor adulterers, nor those who participate in homosexuality, nor cheats (swindlers and thieves), nor greedy graspers, nor drunkards, nor foulmouthed revilers and slanderers, nor extortioners and robbers, will inherit or have any share in the kingdom of God. (1 Cor. 6:9-10 Amplified Bible)

The wicked will not inherit the kingdom of God. No one can live an immoral life and expect to share in the kingdom of God. You will not be able to tap into it now or then. The result of habitual sinning is spiritual death. Let us look at some of the sinful acts mentioned in this scripture. What are "greedy graspers?" We can live moral lives but if we are "greedy graspers," God will not let us into the kingdom. We must share with others and so that we can say, "None of this belongs to me—it all belongs to God." **It all belongs to God!** If you loan someone money and the person does not pay it back, the person did not steal your money. The person stole God's money.

Dealing With Our Addictions

We must first deal with the acknowledgement of the addiction. Many times when we think about addiction, we think about drugs, alcohol, and cigarettes, but there is also pornography that is prevalent among children. Pornography is an addiction, and many times we do not deal with it as an addiction.

We also have people who are addicted to sex. There are many who believe that marriage will be a cure for sexual addiction. Marriage will never be a cure! It may temporarily be an escape to make things a little bit easier, but the sexual addiction is still there. We have thought of sex as being totally legalized once we are married, and it is, but it is still an addiction. Rather than to honor the one that you are with, the man or the woman is the abuser of it. Whether it is a drug, a cigarette, alcohol, sex, pornography, or an eating habit, it is not easy to stop. We **have to kill the problem at the root!**

Alcoholics Anonymous will tell you to first acknowledge you are there. Most people call it the first step to being free, but it is only the entryway. The thing that most people call the first step God said was the introduction to your freedom because it brought you to understand your location. This is exactly how God dealt with Adam.

Remember what God said to Adam when he and Eve were caught in their sin? Has God ever asked you a question? Understand this: Anytime God asks you a question, He already has the answer. He merely wants to bring you to a place of location. God is trying to put you on point.

Now the serpent was more subtil than any beast of the field which the Lord God had made. And he said unto the woman, Yea, hath God said, Ye shall not eat of every tree of the garden? And the woman said unto the serpent, we may eat of the fruit of the trees of the garden: But of the fruit of the tree which is in the midst of the garden, God hath said, Ye shall not eat of it, neither shall ye touch it, lest ye die. And the serpent said unto the woman, Ye shall not surely die: For God doth know that in the day ye eat thereof, then your eyes shall be opened, and ye shall be as gods, knowing good and evil. And when the woman saw that the tree was good for food, and that it was pleasant to the eyes, and a tree to be desired to make one wise, she took of the fruit thereof, and did eat, and gave also unto her husband with her; and he did eat. (Gen. 3:1-6)

Let us look at the process of making decisions. If we can understand this process, we will never again go after something that God really does not want us to have. **Every decision that we make has either a promise or a penalty attached to it.** First the Enemy will trick us into thinking there is no penalty to disobedience; Genesis 3:4 says, *"And the serpent said unto the woman, Ye shall not surely die."* The Devil was convincing Eve that there would be no pain or suffering if she chose to sin. Second, the Enemy will show you how pleasant it is before you go after it. Eve saw that the tree was good for food and "pleasant to the eye." Third, the Enemy plants desire; it was a tree to be desired. Once desire has come into your heart, then you take hold of it. What do you desire to go after that God does not want you to have? You must now check what is in your heart to make sure that what you desire is coming from the Lord. How can you identify incorrect desires? Figure out what made you think that they are good! What caused your desire?

Desire is in the heart and not in the eyes! However, your eyes will create an image for you and put that image in your heart, and then you start desiring what you do not need. Some of the things that we desire are shown to us on television. During a football game and right before halftime, popcorn and hotdogs may appear on the screen before you so that at halftime you will already know what you are going after. Why? The advertisers showed it to you so you would desire it! Just before, during, and after a movie they may show you a scrumptious pizza with cheese. At the bottom of the screen they display the name "Pizza Hut." Now you know where to go to get it! You are not going to call Domino's Pizza or some other pizza place because the television said "Pizza Hut." So immediately after the movie you are going to run to Pizza Hut to get your pizza before the next movie comes on. They may also show seductive scenes from a movie so that you will call "pay for view" and order that particular movie. What you saw created desire in your heart that made you pay for something that you really should not see. **That is only the beginning! The Devil has a plan!** The Devil is not concerned with whether or not you want to pay for it because he will give it to you free. Why? Because he is banking on your becoming addicted!

When the woman saw that the tree was good for food and that it was pleasant to the eye, she took the fruit and ate and then gave it to her husband and he ate. A person engaging in addictive habits likes to do so with other individuals. There are folks who do not want to drink by themselves. Even if you have an addiction going to clubs, you do not want to go by yourself, so you change leagues and jump from the Lord's side to the Devil's side! You are now the ambassador for the Devil! The same folks paint a picture for you, saying, "Don't you want to go with me to the club tonight? Remember that person we saw at the club the last time? Wasn't he off the hook?" You are now off to the club to pursue the image in your head. But you can control your desires by controlling what you are looking at and controlling your thinking. You cannot stop it from coming into your mind, but you can stop it from staying there.

And the eyes of them both were opened, and they knew that they were naked; and they sewed fig leaves, and made themselves aprons. And they heard the voice of the Lord God walking in the garden in the cool of the day: and Adam and his

wife hid themselves from the presence of the Lord God amongst the trees of the garden. And the Lord God called unto Adam, and said unto him, Where art thou? And he said, I heard thy voice in the garden, and I was afraid, because I was naked; and hid myself. And he said, who told thee that thou wast naked? Hast thou eaten of the tree, whereof I commanded thee that thou shouldest not eat? And the man said, The woman whom thou gavest to be with me, she gave me of the tree, and I did eat. And the Lord God said unto the woman, What is this that thou hast done? And the woman said, the serpent beguiled me, and I did eat. And the Lord God said unto the serpent, because thou hast done this, thou art cursed above all cattle, and above every beast of the field; upon thy belly shalt thou go, and dust shalt thou eat all the days of thy life. (Gen. 3:7-14)

God asked Adam, *"Where art thou?"* Before God could make the sacrifice for Adam and Eve, He had to know where they were, and they had to acknowledge their whereabouts. In order for change to happen, you must give your location. Many times we are not honest about our location, saying, "I don't have that problem." The sad thing is that we are not lying; the truth is we do not know where we are. We have been covering up and hiding for a long time. **Deal with your addictive behavior! Come out of hiding!** If you want to break the addiction on your life, you will have to know where you are. Apostle Paul said in 1 Corinthians 2:2, *"For I determined not to know any thing among you, save Jesus Christ, and him crucified."* In other words, God has to send someone to put us on point! We must know when we are lost! Sometimes we can be lost and not know it. Have you ever started out on a trip and ended up far from your destination? You did not know that you were lost until you saw a sign. You knew where you wanted to go but did not know your location.

The Conversion of Paul

When apostle Paul was yet Saul, there was a moment when he had to admit that he was lost. While he was on the road to Damascus with authority from the governing officials to persecute or kill anyone who preached about Jesus Christ, the Lord knocked Paul off his donkey. God asked him, *"Saul, Saul, why persecutest thou me?"* Paul asked, **"Who art thou, Lord?"** He was getting on point! He was getting ready to measure himself.

Let us for a moment use the Muslims as an example. Do you know who they believe the Lord to be? They believe Him to be Elijah Mohammed! Do you know whom they call God? They call Him Allah—which is not necessarily an off name if you really look in the Hebrew language. The name is basically called "the Almighty God." There is nothing wrong with that, but there is something wrong with recognizing Elijah as Lord or the Messiah. Muslims of old believed that Elijah was Lord, and most of them were sincere, but they were "sincerely wrong." **Jesus Christ is Lord!** Elijah died one day but he never got up! However, we serve a risen Lord! **Jesus Christ died and He got up!**

The Muslims believe that they know who the Lord is. However, they don't. They fight the one that we (believers) say is Lord. In order for them to be set on point, they need to find someone who knows Him— not someone who knows of Him but someone who actually knows Him as Lord and Savior.

Paul believed that he was correct, but he was incorrect at the time. As a result, he was persecuting and killing people for preaching the gospel. The Lord answered Paul's question, *"Who art thou, Lord?"* and said, *"I am Jesus whom thou persecutest..."* Paul did not know it at that time, but he was identifying his location so that he would get the attention and help that he needed. He needed salvation but did not know it. Most of us live deeply in denial and cannot be helped until we realize where we are. Denial keeps many of us from our blessings and deliverance.

Cain and Abel

In Genesis 4, Cain brought of the fruit of the ground as an offering unto the Lord, and Abel also brought of the firstlings of his flock and of the fat thereof. The Lord had respect unto Abel and to his offering, but unto Cain and to his offering He had not respect. Abel's offering was "more excellent" than Cain's because he brought the very best. Cain was very angry and his countenance fell. Instead of falling on his knees, he chose to kill his brother, who was in right standing with the Lord.

Whenever you are living in denial, you will deal with the situation either inwardly or outwardly. If you deal with it outwardly, you become callous and attack that which is right. Why? You are in denial. Why get angry with someone else for something that you did that was not right? Have you ever had this to happen to you? If so, check yourself out. Cain was wrong because he did not offer up to God that which was correct. God said to Cain, *"If you have given correctly, would not your offering been received?"* He also told Cain that because he did not give correctly, sin lieth at the door waiting for him to come out. Did he know what was correct? Yes, he did. If he had not known that it was correct, then God would not have put the demand on him when it was time to reward him. We serve a just God.

Have you ever had your flesh scream out loud when the Word of God was going forth? It meant that your flesh was getting hit hard. If you find yourself thinking, "I wish He would shut up," then respond correctly so that your flesh will not give you any more problems.

What is denial? Denial is the act of denying or saying "no" to a request or demand; a contradiction; a statement of an opposition to another; a person who operates in denial, trying to protect himself or herself from the hurt cycle; or an unconscious thought process whereby one alleviates anxiety by refusing to acknowledge the existence of a certain unpleasant aspect of external reality or of one's thoughts or feelings.

How many people are living in denial? What is going

on within you that causes you to hastily contradict or express dissent? Many times we have no clue where we are. Therefore, it is mandatory that we be submitted to someone who will watch over our soul so that we will not have to live in denial. If the man of God says that you are off, then you are off! If you immediately contradict it, what will happen? You will eliminate God from ever speaking to you about the issue. If the person is wrong about you, then God will deal with that person.

Joseph Has a Dream

In Genesis 37, Joseph had a dream and alienated his family, particularly his brothers. He first told his brothers about a dream that he had, and they immediately came against him. They left no room for God to ever speak to them. When he told his father about the dream, his father rebuked him but considered the matter.

Jesus' Pilgrimage To Jerusalem

In Luke 2:41, when Jesus was twelve years old, He and His parents went to Jerusalem for the Feast of the Passover. After the feast, as they started on their way home, Jesus lingered behind in Jerusalem. After a day's journey His parents realized that He was not with them and returned to Jerusalem seeking Him. After three days they found Him in the temple sitting in the midst of the teachers. His mother asked, *"Son, why have you done this to us?"* He replied, *"Why did you seek me?*

Did you not know that I must be about my Father's business?" Even though He was rebuked, which was necessary at that moment because He was still under their authority, Mary considered what He said because God had spoken to her about Jesus' destiny. She did not come up against Him and not hear. Joseph got in on his destiny because he was connected to Mary.

We must be completely honest with ourselves. Sometimes being honest with yourself hurts your flesh because your spirit man is in touch with the destiny that God is moving you in. Your flesh will say, "Let's just stay right here; we are comfortable; we don't need anymore; we don't need to change." Examine yourself. What do you do when you get upset? **This is when your addiction kicks in!** Do you reach for a cigarette, a drink, or a weed? Are you addicted to "yelling" the wrong thing? Do you eat? An emotional reaction requires a response that will be either a right or a wrong response. Either one can lead you to an addiction. There are both good and bad addictions. In your process of getting angry or getting lonely, monitor exactly what you are doing. If your first response is dialing on the phone, it could lead to a bad addiction. It could lead to hell. There is a starting point and there is a destiny. **I can't speak for you, but I have heaven on my mind!**

How Eve Was Deceived

What did the Enemy do to Eve to persuade her to partake of what was forbidden? The Enemy does not know any new tricks! The same old tricks are done in different ways. Genesis 3:2-3 says, *"And the woman said unto the serpent, We may eat of the fruit of the trees of the garden: But of the fruit of the tree which is in the midst of the garden, God hath said, Ye shall not eat of it, neither shall ye touch it, lest ye die."*

Every time we sin, something dies, and we suffer pain. For example, God warns heavy drinkers over and over again about drinking, but the warnings do not deter them from drinking continuously. The consequence of their drinking could be their being involved in a car accident and hitting a tree (pain). What is God saying up front? Don't drink! Drinking is a mocker. Proverbs 20:1 says, *"Wine is a mocker, strong drink a brawler, and whoever is led astray by it is not wise." (NSRV) Pain is applied to every sin.*

How Prophecy Is Handled

Have you ever had a prophecy given to you and not known whether to receive it or not? Take these steps to decide whether to accept it or not. First, if what was said to you does not apply to you, reject it! Second, if you are not sure of the prophecy, then hear it and consider the matter. Third, if the prophecy given is correct and accurate, receive it and nurture it! Fourth, if the prophecy renders you guilty and God has convicted you, admit it! **Know this: God convicts you long before you even receive the prophecy!**

Many times we think that our "mess" won't come out on the forefront, but it will! Someone will catch you in that lottery line! It may well be Mary and Lucy who have the loose lips and will tell the whole church about it! Don't get messed up when someone puts your business in the street. Why? Because God warned you long before it got out! But even after it is out, there is still hope for you if you are breathing. You serve a God of "another chance" and not a "second chance." Most of us need more than a "second chance." **Admit it and quit it! The same formula must be used for an addiction!** Admit that you have the addiction. **Warning:** You cannot admit it to just anyone! If you admit it to the wrong person, your business will be broadcast throughout the church, through the street, and to anyone who will listen. This is the reason you should know who your spiritual father or spiritual mother is! You need to know who your pastor is and who covers you so that you will know where to run. You do not run away from them when you sin—you run to them! If you are addicted to something, you had better run to your man or woman of God and have that thing destroyed!

Chapter 2

Threefold Relationship

The Triune Protection of God

Through God-given relationships, God has provided us with the power and ability to defeat the Enemy. Relationships are not to hinder us but rather to protect us. If we learn the purpose for which relationships are created, there will be no room for abuse. There are three facets of relationship that God has given us as protective mechanisms. They are prayer, worship, and the Word. Remember that God did everything in threes. The three that bear record in heaven are the Father, the Son, and the Holy Ghost. The three that bear witness on earth are the spirit, the water, and the blood. The triune protection of God is also threefold: God-ward relationship, brother and sister relationship, and spousal relationship.

God-ward Relationship

Your God-ward relationship is designed to bring you into a place of intimacy with God. Do you have a close relationship with God? The first person that we need to establish a relationship with is God. Most of us are trying to fill needs and voids. Something inside you desires to be filled with God. God-ward relationship has three components that must be kept strong to ward off the Enemy. The three areas are:

Prayer—Your communication with God
Worship—Your yielding to God
Word—Your direction in God

God-ward relationship is God's plan to bring you into a healthy place. Many people go to psychics because they do not have a prayer life. God wants us to pray. The next component is worship, coming into an intimate place with God. Many people try to find intimacy with other people, so they are unable to see what God has for them. But we yearn for intimacy because God is pulling on us to worship. God is saying, **I need you to become closer to me!** God then leads us into the Word for direction. The Word of God will get you out of your problems.

Brother and Sister Relationship

Many times we try to get around this relationship because we think that we are not in dire need of that brother or sister. I have three questions to ask you. To whom are you accountable? With whom do you commune? With whom are you so in love? We need that brother or sister to sharpen us in three areas. These three areas are:

Love—Agape (unconditional) and Phileo (brotherly)
Communion—Koinonia or fellowship
Accountability—Being responsible or liable to

someone

Agape love

Unconditional love is what God wants us to have in this pure brother and sister relationship. We must know where to draw the line in this brother-to-brother and sister-to-sister relationship. In this relationship, we enter a place of love with them, but it is agape love. Often we end up coming to a place in our relationship with a brother or sister where God never intended. As a result, it becomes perverted love.

Phileo or brotherly love

God has no problem with a brother-to-brother, a brother-to-sister, a sister-to-sister, or a sister-to-brother relationship, as long you know where to draw the line. Keep it pure!

Koinonia or fellowship

This is a relationship in which you actually commune with your brother or sister.

Accountability

We may have the love and communion together, but we do not always have the accountability together. Why? Because it means that we must become responsible or liable for someone. Who is it that corrects you, or have you set up yourself to be corrected by anyone? **You should have a brother or sister who will put you in check!** God establishes that brother and sister relationship so that we can be accountable to someone. **You can't tell everybody your stuff.**

These are qualities that one needs to possess in relationship to our brother and sister. It will mean the difference between your being married or not married.

Spousal Relationship

When you are in the brother and sister relationship, there is a very important facet that enhances your ability to be committed to your spouse. This facet is accountability. If you are unable to be accountable to a brother or sister, then you will never be able to exemplify the kind of commitment that God is looking for in a marriage. What about communion in a marriage? How many husbands or wives cannot talk to each other? Your spouse should be your best friend. If he or she is not, then you are at a very vulnerable place! Are you on your way to marriage? If you are in a relationship with someone who is not your best friend now, then that person will not be your best friend later. **You must be able to commune with the person!** This relationship is the act of sharing one's intimate thoughts and emotions with another.

God gives us the brother-to-brother or sister-to-sister relationship so that we may go to the next level of relationship. Make sure that you have in place the God-ward relationship, the brother and sister relationship, and the spousal relationship. The reason for the relationships is that we can stay at a committed place with God, a committed place with a brother or sister, and a committed place with our spouse. The next step to breaking addictions and strongholds is an all-out surrender.

Chapter 3

Steps to Changing Bad Habits That Create Addictions

The first step in being set free from something is receiving education about it. Without the knowledge, you won't know what to be set free from. Some of us come from dysfunctional backgrounds and homes, and we have nothing to measure by to know where we are. We could be totally off base about particular things and not know it.

Step 1. Surrender

The first step to breaking every addiction and bondage is to surrender. Surrender enables God to step in. If we operate in denial and fail to see our part in any given situation, we tie God's hands and don't allow Him to heal us. We are so stuck in the "I" syndrome that we can't see what God wants to accomplish. The word "surrender" means to yield to the power of another; give up under compulsion; relinquish; or give up or yield oneself or the possession of one thing to another. We know surrender is easy because we are quick to do it when we want to. So just give up! Let go! You must surrender to the Lord and to the power of His hand. We must believe that once we come to a place of "giving up," He is able to hold us up. An acknowledgement of your location is extremely important if you are to come to a full surrender. The problem is that some of us "partially" surrender. When God comes into your life, He has already broken the power on whatever the addiction is, but you are holding on with one hand. Before you can be free from your addiction, you must surrender to the Lord and the power of His hand.

Romans 8:2 says, **"For the law of the Spirit of life in Christ Jesus hath made me free from the law of sin and death."** God accomplished what the law could not do by sending His only begotten son, Jesus, to die and set us free from the penalty of sin and death. The law of the Spirit of life is working to free you from addictions and bondages.

Once you move into an addictive behavior, its forces will try to overpower and restrain you. When we are bound, the Enemy tries to hold us right where we are. Though we give up things when we are saved, there is always that one thing that we are unable let go. I call it the "thorn in my flesh." It did not come from God but from the messenger of Satan, who sent it to buffet my flesh. In 2 Corinthians 12:7-9, Paul says, *"... there was given to me a thorn in the flesh, the messenger of Satan to buffet me... I besought the Lord thrice, that it might depart from me ... My grace is sufficient for thee: for my strength is made perfect in weakness."* God expects us to deal with things that are working against us. Where you are weak, God's power strengthens you. God will not touch that one area that you are struggling with. God says, "I have dealt with everything else, so now you need to ride on my empowering grace." **You will have to do it yourself,**

and He will grow you to handle it. We must look outside ourselves and turn to God. **We must surrender to His power!**

Saul's Conversion and Surrender

Let us look at what Saul did in order to begin his freedom in the Lord from his addictive behavior against the work and Word of the Lord. Saul of Tarsus had persecuted and killed many Jews. He had gotten official papers from the high priest in Jerusalem to go to Damascus and bring back disciples so that they could stand trial by the Sanhedrin council. In John 16, Christ warned the disciples about the hatred they would encounter for His sake. John 16:2 says, *"... the time cometh, that whosoever killeth you will think that he doeth God service."*

They will kill you and think that they did God a favor! That is not God! The people who did this were sincere. The trouble is that they were "sincerely wrong." Saul asked a question that set him free forever. On the road to Damascus he had an encounter with the Lord. God knocked him off his donkey and asked, "Saul, Saul, why persecutest thou me?" The first question that Saul asked the Lord was, **"Who are you, Lord?"** It is imperative that we know who the deliverer is if we are to obtain what He has.

In this season, God stands ready to free us from the bondage that holds us if we will just acknowledge Him. It is God's great desire to use us for His glory. Saul then asked the Lord, *"What will you have me to do?"* **He accepted his conversion and his call in the same**

day! Saul already thought he was working for the Lord —but he was not! **He surrendered!** That was the second thing that Saul had to do in order to become free. If Saul had not done what he had been instructed to do, then that would have been recognized as a **"verbal surrender"** and not a **"heartfelt surrender."** Most of us have "verbal surrender." **You relinquish everything when there is a heartfelt surrender!** You relinquish every facet of your being and rely totally on the Lord and His leading.

We are to yield totally to whatever God tells us to do, which could be a struggle because we have been led by our soul for so long. If you have to know before you can trust, then you will always be stuck in your addiction. We must understand the system by which God operates. The system is a system of faith. That is to trust even when you can't trace it. God says in Isaiah 55:8-9, **"For my thoughts are not your thoughts, neither are my ways your ways, saith the Lord. For as the heavens are higher than the earth, so are my ways higher than your ways, and my thoughts than your thoughts."**

What Are Your Thoughts?
This is the greatest area where the Enemy will try to trip us up. What you think about before you go to bed will determine what your thoughts will be the next morning. I commit to memory most of the scriptures at night before retiring to bed. Before I turn the lights out, I commit the book, chapter, and verse, word for word, and then I repeat it over and over again. When I awaken the next morning, that scripture is

fresh in my mind.

What if you did that every day of the year? At the end of the year you would know at least 365 scriptures out of the Bible Your key thought at night becomes the manifestation of your next day. Many of us go to sleep with the television on, and whatever is on, whether good or bad, is being fed into our spirit. It wouldn't hurt to have a Word tape going while you are sleeping! Your inner man is always listening to what is around you while you're sleep. Don't ever forget that your thoughts form an image within you. Therefore, whatever image you form within yourself becomes what you fulfill later. One of the most powerful vehicles on the earth is the mind that has the ability to form an image. Once that image is formed, you are then on your way toward manifestation in the negative or the positive.

You have the ability to manifest healing and deliverance from your addictions just as fast as you can manifest the image that carries you toward sin and defeat.

It takes some surrendering! Watch what you think about tonight so that your tomorrow will be protected! These are various steps to help you break addictive behavior. Some people kill their tomorrow by not controlling their thoughts at night. What is it that God wants to do for you tomorrow that you killed the night before? There is a price to be paid when we sin!

Finally, my brethren, be strong in the Lord, and in the power of his might. Put on the whole armour of God, that ye may be able to stand against the wiles of the Devil. For we wrestle not against flesh and blood, but against principalities, against powers, against the rulers of the darkness of this world, against spiritual wickedness in high places. Wherefore take unto you the whole armour of God, that ye may be able to withstand in the evil day, and having done all, to stand. (Eph. 6:10-13)

The Devil has a method of bringing you into bondage, and he will follow your blueprint. In Genesis 3, Eve saw, desired, took, and gave. The Devil had a method in mind before he ever showed the tree to her. The Devil watches your every move, he sees what exactly turns you on, and then he sets you up. If food is what will set you up and he knows that you like fried chicken, potatoes, and gravy, then he is not going to come to you with black-eyed peas.

Let me give you some Word on this—remember Cain? In Genesis 4:6-7, the Word says, **"And the Lord said unto Cain, Why art thou wroth? And why is thy countenance fallen? If thou doest well, shalt thou not be accepted? and if thou doest not well, sin lieth at the door. And unto thee shall be his desire, and thou shalt rule over him."** Satan was crouching at the door waiting for Cain to make the wrong move. What can we do? **We can't tell Satan to go to hell because he isn't there!** But even though it is not time for him to go there yet, we can remind him of his destiny. He keeps telling you things, so you keep reminding him where he is going one day. Know this: God is omnipresent—He is everywhere at the same time, but the Devil cannot be. The Devil will send a demonic force to put Satanic pressure on the church. He uses your addiction against you because that is the only thing that he has on you.

Jesus says in John 14:30, *"Hereafter I will not talk much with you: for the prince of this world cometh, and hath nothing in me."* Let us repeat the very words that Jesus said. The wicked one has nothing in you! He has no link in you! You can say with authority, "There is no sin in me, there is no offense in me, and there is nothing that the Enemy owns that is in me." We have apostolic authority over demons, and all we have to do is to open our mouth and say what God says! We have the authority and power over the Devil and over the darkness, and the only thing that we have to do is to rise up and say what God says!

For though we walk (live) in the flesh, we are not carrying on our warfare according to the flesh and using mere human weapons. For the weapons of our warfare are not physical [weapons of flesh and blood], but they are mighty before God for the overthrow and destruction of strongholds, [Inasmuch as we] refute arguments and theories and reasonings and every proud and lofty thing that sets itself up against the [true] knowledge of God; and we lead every thought and purpose away captive into the obedience of Christ (the Messiah, the Anointed One), Being in readiness to punish

every [insubordinate for his] disobedience, when
your own submission and obedience [as a church]
are fully secured and complete. (2 Cor. 10:3-6
Amplified Bible)

When someone asks you to pray for him, you do not
have to bring him to the elders or ministers—you have
apostolic authority so you pray for him!

Bridging the Gap for the Family

There is a great need for intercessors to rise up
in the body of Christ because of the attacks and
sin that have entered the body of Christ. We have
been talking about the family and its purpose in the
world; there is also a great attack against it. If there
comes a great rising of the intercessor in the church,
then there will also arise a power so great that it will
shake the very foundation of anything that seems to
hold the church. God is calling all of us back to a place
of prayer. God is also calling all the intercessors back
to a place of activation. Let's come back to the
gathering place for the purpose of **"bridging the
gap."**

And the word of the LORD came unto me,
saying, Son of man, say unto her, Thou art the
land that is not cleansed, nor rained upon in the
day of indignation. There is a conspiracy of her
prophets in the midst thereof, like a roaring lion
ravening the prey; they have devoured souls; they
have taken the treasure and precious things; they
have made her many widows in the midst thereof.
Her priests have violated my law, and have

profaned mine holy things: they have put no difference between the holy and profane, neither have they shewed difference between the unclean and the clean, and have hid their eyes from my sabbaths, and I am profaned among them. Her princes in the midst thereof are like wolves ravening the prey, to shed blood, and to destroy souls, to get dishonest gain. And her prophets have daubed them with untempered morter, seeing vanity, and divining lies unto them, saying, Thus saith the Lord GOD, when the LORD hath not spoken. The people of the land have used oppression, and exercised robbery, and have vexed the poor and needy: yea, they have oppressed the stranger wrongfully. And I sought for a man among them, that should make up the hedge, and stand in the gap before me for the land, that I should not destroy it: but I found none. Therefore have I poured out mine indignation upon them; I have consumed them with the fire of my wrath: their own way have I recompensed upon their heads, saith the Lord GOD. (Ezek. 22:23-31)

In this text the Lord is speaking against the prophets and priests for not obeying, for polluting, and for speaking when God had not spoken. God wanted to remedy their condition and not be forced to destroy them. "**And I sought for a man among them.**" God is always looking for someone who is among them in the city, country, church, or family, or for someone **attached to it** to make **intercession for it.** You cannot be **detached from it** and make **intercession for it.**

Gap Relationship #1—Stay among those you're reaching.

If you are willing to engage in the assignment, anointing is available. The anointing is for results and not just for a good feeling. God can give you a good feeling any time. If we really want to see good results we must have the anointing in our bridging the gap. I heard an attorney say, "The hardest case to crack is the one that was an inside job." When you stay inside and become faithful, the Devil never will be able to figure out who is the cause of the breakthrough that is happening in what he keeps attacking.

Gap Relationship #2—Be numbered with the transgressors.

Therefore will I divide him a portion with the great, and he shall divide the spoil with the strong; because he hath poured out his soul unto death: and he was numbered with the transgressors; and he bare the sin of many, and made intercession for the transgressors.(Isa. 53:12)

Inasmuch as the Enemy is shrewd in his attack against the church, we the intercessors must be just as shrewd in fighting back and reclaiming the lost. Jesus was numbered with the transgressors and prayed from that standpoint or position. He Himself was not a transgressor, but He never defended Himself when accused. If Jesus had defended Himself on the cross, then that would have negated His being able to intercede from that position.

Gap Relationship #3—Intercede that they heed the right voice.

But if they be prophets, and if the word of the LORD be with them, let them now make intercession to the LORD of hosts, that the vessels which are left in the house of the LORD, and in the house of the king of Judah, and at Jerusalem, go not to Babylon. (Jer. 27:18)

In this verse, God wanted them to escape the famine and they did not, but God promised that He would bring them back out and restore them in their own land. If they had heeded the wrong voice, then they would have lost their lives. Through proper intercession, the right decision is always made, and what needs to be heard is always established.

Gap Relationship #4—Yield to the Holy Spirit in Intercession!

Likewise the Spirit also helpeth our infirmities: for we know not what we should pray for as we ought: but the Spirit itself maketh intercession for us with groanings which cannot be uttered. (Rom. 8:26)

The Holy Spirit always knows what to pray for; therefore, if we follow His lead, we will always pray according to the will of God. There is an ability to always do whatever is set before you because the Holy Spirit is always making intercession for you.

It is important to note the phrase "with groanings which cannot be uttered." It is important to have a prayer language because the Enemy cannot break through the prayer code of that language. Yet there are some things that should be prayed in English because you want the Devil to know and hear those things. Through your prayer language there is enough power to totally annihilate the works of any enemy.

Gap Relationship #5—We live to make intercession for them!

Wherefore he is able also to save them to the uttermost that come unto God by him, seeing he ever liveth to make intercession for them. (Heb. 7:25)

This scripture is talking about Jesus and is the same thing that God is saying regarding us. It does the heart of God good when He can say that we ever live to make intercession for the family, saints, church, government, schools, or our co-workers. This moves us into a powerful place of prayer and intercession. Intercession is not only for those who are unsaved but also for the saved. Intercession will launch you into the place of your purpose.

How do you deal with voids in your life?

The fulfilling of every void is God's job! If you feel empty in any way in your life, it is not the responsibility of your wife, husband, or friend to fulfill that need.

Genesis 1:1-2 says, **"In the beginning God created the heaven and earth. And the earth was without form, and void...."** When we say "void," we are talking about "empty." Many of you have said, "There are periods in my life when I feel empty." Whenever we feel empty, we tend to want to put something or somebody in that place, and if we do not get a sense of fulfillment, we feel like pulling our hair out! **But filling voids is God's job!** In the beginning God created the heaven and earth. Therefore, God is the author of every single thing that is in the earth. *"And the spirit of God moved upon the face of the waters."* So God moves upon that which is empty. We must place our dependence on God so that He can bring fulfillment to that empty place. God knows what fits there, and we don't. We do not understand why we enter into sexual relations, drink excessively, or get involved in other addictions in order to fulfill a void. We must deal with this or we will continue to make the same mistakes.

Some people cannot get by one night of loneliness. What is loneliness? It is a void! You have always been accustomed to having someone there, and then you try to grab anyone wearing jeans or perfume. We try to put things in that empty place. We reach for familiar things. What is familiar? If I am lonely and if you are lonely, then we reach for someone who is lonely. If we both are lonely, there is a great drawing in that situation.

Tremendous problems come when we try to fill our own void because we do not know what goes there. You are not capable of doing God's job! We get saved, sanctified, Holy Ghost filled, and fire baptized, we have got Jesus on our mind, and we are running for our lives, and all of a sudden we do not have good sense. How many people do you hear discussing whether they have the right mate or not? You don't hear folks talking about that in the world—we start talking about it when we get saved. That is the reason there is such a high rate of divorce in the church world. We say, "I don't think I have the right one," or "I don't think this is the one that the Lord gave me." The truth of the matter is the Lord does not give anyone a mate. However, the Lord does present a mate to you! It is your choice as to whether or not you want to receive.

God did not make Adam keep Eve. He created her, and then He presented her. Adam could have said, "No, thank you." When God created everything that He was going to put on the earth, there was nothing compatible for Adam, so there was a void in him.

The Causes of Voids

What causes voids? It could be a relationship gone sour, or the loss of an item that you loved so much, or a missing loved one who has passed on to be with the Lord. We get involved in all kinds of things and make these things into gods. Could your relationship with that person, your loss of that item, or your relationship with that loved one possibly be idol worship? At the point of loss you must look back to God, who is the giver of what you lost. God is the author and finisher of everything.

Idol worship is an image of a god used as an object or instrument of worship, or an object of ardent or excessive devotion or admiration. How many of us fit that description? How many of us have an excessive devotion or admiration for a particular thing or person? I have witnessed individuals who were involved in accidents who loved their cars so much that they were ready to fight. How many of us are ready to put on the gloves because someone touched our relationship or because our idol was not accepted? This is idol worship! God said, "Thou shall have no other gods before me." There are folks who are jealous of their loved ones to the point of idol worship. Where is the line drawn between whether or not it is an authentic jealousy that we are supposed to have versus its being excessive to the point of idol worship? This is where you must find the line and draw it! Know this: When we come into the place, we bring God with us! The object is not holy; God is holy! Do you know what is fascinating? Women who have fingernail polish on can lay hands on the sick and they will recover. There are some churches that would call you unsaved if you have fingernail polish on your fingernails.

Step 2. Closing Old Doors

Too many times we keep doors of the past open to things that we never want to show up in the future. Consider the cost of leaving old doors open. We can never come into the new if we fail to close the old.

Remember Not the Former Things

Remember ye not the former things, neither consider the things of old. Behold, I will do a new thing; now it shall spring forth; shall ye not know it? I will even make a way in the wilderness, and rivers in the desert. (Isa. 43:18-19)

We must forget the former things and not dwell on the past. There is too much in the past that will cause havoc if we continue to remember. God always takes you beyond the past in order to establish the new. It is important that you close doors correctly. If not, there is certainty of bondages and addiction coming in some form.

Closing Doors to Past Relationships

Leaving things open creates the opportunity for others things to come in. People who have been divorced or have been in a bad relationship might remarry and never close old doors. People who don't close marriages properly and divorce will no doubt create an addiction that will cause bad relationships. They will inevitably bring their old baggage into a new relationship. People carry bondages from one marriage to another and never realize where the problem got started. They will leave one marriage having never gotten over the person whom they were married to. It is not that there is such a big problem in their present marriage, but rather that they brought a third party into the marriage covenant. The person who has all of the issues enters into a relationship with one who has never been married and who has never been in a bad relationship, and eventually that person will end up with a hole in his or her heart, become damaged emotionally, and not know what to do. What is the damage done here? All of the unresolved issues from one person's former relationship have now been attached to the other person, and now there is a void in his or her life. The marriage covenant was solidified at the altar with two people. Yet in this covenant there is a third party that the spouse is not aware of. The person who has not closed the last relationship properly cannot give this new person a chance because only one person can occupy someone's heart at a time. Therefore, when you have not closed a relationship properly, there is someone else that actually lives there. **Anything that you get into you must end correctly!**

Bonding

When a man and a woman are joined together, their hearts and emotions become so knitted and bonded that everybody becomes affected when they are pulled apart. There is an intertwining of your heart and the individual's heart, or maybe you are connected by your souls. But when you later get involved with a new relationship, you have to resolve the issues from the old relationship or else a part of what was on that former partner and the part that is already on you will transfer to that new individual.

It is important that we cleanse ourselves from the effects of the other person. Once you are bonded, if it doesn't work, you cannot take it back and make someone else pay for it! When two people are so in love with each other, and then something just does not go right, all of a sudden one of them does not want to be with the other anymore. When they finally pull apart, they have so much of each other on them, and one of them ends up with a void, a hole, or an empty spot inside. Because we do not want to be alone we try to find someone to fit in where that person was. It is not going to work. The void in your life is not fixed but covered up. If the doors have not been properly closed and you get involved with someone else who was all right initially, this person has now come in contact with you who have the void; and once this person finally gets away from you, he or she now has a void. The other person has so much of you, most of the time he or she ends up with what you left. If we have the void filled by God, we can close the door properly.

Why are you lonely? What do you do when you are lonely? More than likely you do not get into the Word. You are praying during that particular period. You are meditating upon the fact that you are by yourself, and then you end up getting spiritual company: the Devil. The physical company comes later. When two people with a void get together, then they put something on each other. What should happen instead is for both to develop a relationship with God.

Seasonal Relationships Many of us get married before we finish being single. Singleness is not necessarily a state of being—it is a season. However, marriage is a season that does not end, and it is also a state of being. In marriage you enter a place, and in singleness you enter only a season. The amazing thing about singleness is that you can't tell it when to start and when to end. Most of us jump on the plane and end that season! If you don't complete your season of singleness before you get married, then you have to complete your season of singleness while you are married.

Ideally you start off single and go from your singleness into another season that is courtship, then from courtship to the espousal state, and then to marriage.

Singleness—You are not really looking for relationship. When you sense that your season of singleness is ending, then you enter courtship.

Courtship—When you enter the period of courtship, you are not trying to hand over a bunch of responsibility. Nothing is really happening between the two of you. You date, you go home, and that is it! When that season starts to end, you enter into the espousal state.

Espousal state—This is when there is a proposal. God does this! He realizes that in the next season you are going to say, "I do." He is not going to let you say, "I do" without your knowing what you are saying, "I do" to. Anyone who ends up getting married may say later, "He sure wasn't like that then." Yes, he was—you were just blind as a bat, and you were not trying to see it!

God is a just God, and He pulls the covers off so that you can see that person for who he or she is. He does this so that you both know what to be working on. When you say, "I do," you say "I do" to everything in that courtship. Just be honest! James Dobson stated that you need to go into a marriage with your eyes wide open. When you get married, you need to close your eyes tight. If you understand the seasons, then you can remain within that one season. Many times we jump into marriage and have to deal with all four seasons in one state of being. You are still learning about that person and you should have learned about that during courtship. You have no clue as to what kind of ice cream he likes or his favorite color. After we are single, we need to close that door and enter the next period.

Jacob and Esau

Let us take a look at the twin sons of Isaac and the struggle within their mother's womb.

And the LORD said unto her, Two nations are in thy womb, and two manner of people shall be separated from thy bowels; and the one people shall be stronger than the other people; and the elder shall serve the younger. (Gen. 25:23)

This prophecy concerning Jacob and Esau brought conflict between the two brothers.

And when her days to be delivered were fulfilled, behold, there were twins in her womb. And the first came out red, all over like an hairy garment; and they called his name Esau. And after

that came his brother out, and his hand took hold on Esau's heel; and his name was called Jacob: and Isaac was threescore years old when she bare them. And the boys grew: and Esau was a cunning hunter, a man of the field; and Jacob was a plain man, dwelling in tents. And Isaac loved Esau, because he did eat of his venison: but Rebekah loved Jacob. (Gen. 25:24-28)

Isaac loved Esau and Rebekah loved Jacob. The parents favored one child over the other. The problem was that the mother loved Jacob so much that she decided to help God out. **We do not have to help God out!** God had already prophesied that the older would serve the younger. Favoritism set the stage for further conflict and deception. There was never closure because Rebekah's deceptive ways were never closed properly.

And Rebekah spake unto Jacob her son, saying, Behold, I heard thy father speak unto Esau thy brother, saying, Bring me venison, and make me savoury meat, that I may eat, and bless thee before the LORD before thy death. (Gen. 27:6-7)

If you move from one relationship to another, until you deal with it you will never stop running. Deal with it! **Don't hold grudges—make peace!** Romans 12:18 says, *"If it be possible, as much as lieth in you, live peaceably with all men."* Live peaceably with them inasmuch as possible. Do your part even if they mislead you when you go back. There are tremendous rewards when you do your part. Even if they did not receive, leave the Word with them so that God can work in them.

And Esau hated Jacob because of the blessing wherewith his father blessed him: and Esau said in his heart, The days of mourning for my father are at hand; then will I slay my brother Jacob. And these words of Esau her elder son were told to Rebekah: and she sent and called Jacob her younger son, and said unto him, Behold, thy brother Esau, as touching thee, doth comfort himself, purposing to kill thee. Now therefore, my son, obey my voice; and arise, flee thou thou to Laban my brother to Haran. (Gen. 27:41-43)

Esau purposed in his heart to kill his brother Jacob after the death of his father. Jacob's mother had told him what Esau had said. She now had to send him away for fear for his life. How many of us have ever experienced anything like this before or have purposed in your heart to get revenge on someone? This puts us right back to idol worship because we would rather harm someone else than see our fault in the matter.

And Jacob sod pottage: and Esau came from the field, and he was faint: And Esau said to Jacob, Feed me, I pray thee, with that same red pottage; for I am faint: therefore was his name called Edom. And Jacob said, Sell me this day thy birthright. And Esau said, Behold, I am at the point to die: and what profit shall this birthright do to me? And Jacob said, Swear to me this day; and he sware unto him: and he sold his birthright unto

Jacob. (Gen. 25:29-33)

Esau stated that Jacob cheated him out of his birthright. He promised revenge. His accusation was not true! He was in denial. It was an even exchange even though it was an unfair one. What would we sell for another bowl of food? Are you able to complete a fast? What would you forfeit because you are not able to make it through? You decided to fast for a whole week, and on the third day of your fast you drove by a fast food restaurant and asked the Lord for forgiveness because you were about to have a supreme pizza. You indulged, but what did you forfeit? If you suffer with Him, you will reign with Him.

Don't Leave Your Job Incorrectly

People who don't leave jobs correctly will inevitably leave another job incorrectly. Whatever you fail to close correctly will start a pattern in your life.

KEY THOUGHT
All patterns (whatever you do over and over) turn into addictions or addictive behavior.

Anything you do for a period of twenty-one days turns into a habit. Whatever habit you have and want to get rid of, I dare you to shut it down for forty days! Why forty days? Forty is a number for supernatural. **Supernatural results will happen if you do something for forty days!**

Jesus fulfills His time and closes it properly

And he came to Nazareth, where he had been brought up: and, as his custom was, he went into the synagogue on the Sabbath day, and stood up for to read. And there was delivered unto him the book of the prophet Esaias. And when he had opened the book, he found the place where it was written, The Spirit of the Lord is upon me because he hath anointed me to preach the gospel to the poor; he hath sent me to heal the brokenhearted, to preach deliverance to the captives, and recovering of sight to the blind, to set at liberty them that are bruised, To preach the acceptable year of the Lord. And he closed the book, and he gave it again to the minister, and sat down. And the eyes of all of them that were in the synagogue were fastened on him. (Luke 4:16-20)

Jesus was closing an era of time correctly! He opened the book and found His place; announced it to the officials; closed the book; and sat down prior to making His exit. It is absolutely amazing to me how addictions are formed. Any addiction can be avoided by one simple rule—end or exit everything properly by stating why you must exit to those in authority or those involved.

When God is involved in what you end, His major reason is that He wants to do a new thing. The word "new" means that which is unfamiliar, different from the former, or modern. If you never close that which you are familiar with, God can never bring you into the new or unfamiliar.

Matthew 5:17 says, *"Think not that I am come to destroy the Law or the prophets: I am not come to destroy but to fulfil."* Jesus in essence was saying that He came to bring fulfillment to it. What does that mean? That means to close it properly and then bring in the new. We by nature are people who do not like change, but God wants to bring us to a place of change so that we may make the next move. God's next move will not be according to our thinking but will far surpass our mental intellect. Then we will be able to see God make a way in the wilderness and rivers in the desert. That only means that God wants to do something that we have not yet seen. God wants to make a way for you in the desert experience that you may be having at this time. When you come to the place of knowing that you cannot back up, stoop down, or quit, then you will know that God is about to do something in your day that you will not believe. If you close things properly, then you will not be enslaved, imprisoned, or trapped by your addiction, and you can hold on to the promises of God. The same power that makes a way through the wilderness is the same power that will cause your new thing to spring forth.

Step 3. Defeating the Enemy at Thought Stage

Many of us allow the Devil free course in our thought life. In order to defeat the Enemy, we must learn to redirect our thinking. If there is a situation in your life in which it seems that you are unable to control, redirect your thinking.

First, we must be honest with ourselves. It becomes very easy to push off our problem on someone else. Many of us blame the past for our problems. Instead of admitting that it is our fault, we place the blame on the fact that we did not have a daddy or we did not have a mama. This may be true, and maybe you did not get certain deposits because they were not there, but get past that now! They may be responsible for hitting you with that trauma, but it is your fault for carrying it.

We must deal with our thought life because the Enemy uses the things we carry to keep us locked up and bound! We are not trying to get out from under the Devil's hold, and yet we continue to blame him for our problems. We must begin to learn how to master the issues in our lives. We must start by asking, "Am I truthful with myself?" Do you deal with your issues and say, "This is my fault"?

For though we walk in the flesh, we do not war after the flesh: (For the weapons of our warfare are not carnal, but mighty through God to the pulling down of strong holds); Casting down imaginations, and every high thing that exalteth itself against the knowledge of God, and bringing into captivity every thought to the obedience of Christ. (2 Cor. 10:3-5)

God has given every believer the ability to pull down

strongholds. Stop overlooking particular things and deal with them! **Nothing is created outside of your thought life!** This is where God started! You must first have an image of what you want before you can declare it. If you have incorrect images inside yourself, you are going to create incorrect objects. Has there ever been a time in your life when you got extremely angry with someone and had pictures of what you were going to do to that person?

For the weapons of our warfare are not physical [weapons of flesh and blood], but they are mighty before God for the overthrow and destruction of strongholds. (2 Cor. 10:4 Amplified Bible)

The weapons of our warfare are not natural weapons but are mighty through God's divine power. We can overthrow and destroy Satan's strongholds. We have the ability to manifest healing and deliverance and come out of our addiction as swiftly as we do when we create an image that carries us toward sin and defeat. Do you have defeat on your mind, or do you have victory on your mind? All you have to do is listen to what you talk about and you will know the answer.

In dealing with biblical studies, one of the laws of sermon preparation is called, "the law of most mention." When reading a biblical story it may not be clear to you if you do not pay attention to what is mentioned most. You outline a certain word or passage that keeps coming up again and again because it will let you know the frame of mind of the speaker. A person will know what is in your mind by what you say the most. If you build a correct image in yourself, then you can wipe out anything that the Devil wants you to do. You must change your thought life.

For many of us, our down moments, depressing moments, and lonely moments are at night. It is at night when your mind begins to settle down and you begin to think on many things. This is the time when you may tell yourself that you are lonely or you may think about what someone did to you during the day and get mad all over again. What you are thinking about is setting an atmosphere.

What should you do? **Fill your mind with the Word!** Try putting on a Word tape before going to sleep. We are talking about what is happening in our lives, but we are not doing anything about it. We are meditating upon what is not going right, and we are not counterattacking it with the Word of God. I have gone to sleep with the television on and dreamt that I was playing the keyboard. The music from the television was going into my ears, and what I heard formed an image as if I were actually doing it myself. Form the correct image. Put the Word on before going to bed, and you could very well dream that you are preaching!

Mark 11:24 says, *"…What things soever ye desire, when ye pray, believe that ye receive them, and ye shall have them." None of that will ever happen until you build an image on the inside! Whatever you are believing God for just build an image on the inside and you will have exactly what you are going after.*

It is easy to get what you are after when you build an image inside! What you think about before you go to bed will determine your thoughts the next morning. You can kill your tomorrow by not controlling your thoughts the night before. If you build an image on the inside, declare that you will receive the manifestation of what you said. **Know this: Your words carry life, and they will form anything that you say!**

There was a member at my former church who was diagnosed with terminal cancer, and the church was believing for that person's healing. The person, on the other hand, was not necessarily believing for his healing because of pain and an image of the worst that could happen. The person died and an autopsy was done. The doctors were astonished because his body did not show the cancer and there was no reason for him to have died, yet he died. He died because he had an image of dying. The church had an image of healing. Neither one contradicted the other! **He died healed!** Regardless of what the situation is, believe you will come out of it.

In Genesis we find that Eve had not mastered the task of defeating the Enemy at thought stage. If we could see the schemes of the Enemy and be sharp enough to immediately reject them, we would be much better off. God has given us the tools to overcome every trick and scheme of the Enemy. The task to defeat him is up to us. Remember that the way to defeat the Enemy is to know how he comes and cut him off before his plan works.

Genesis 3:1 says, *"The serpent was more subtil than any beast of the field...."* What does that tell us? It tells us that the Enemy comes in some slick or sly way. He uses crafty words in order to trip us, persuade us, or discredit something. What did the Devil say to you the last time that you were alone that you did not solicit from him? **When God speaks to you, He says exactly what He means and means exactly what He says!**

Let us look at the Devil's scheme
In Genesis 3:1 the Bible says, *"...hath God said, Ye shall not eat of every tree of the garden?"* The Enemy offered something that had been forbidden by God as an attractive, enticing option. Satan will plant a seemingly innocent question in your mind to cause you to doubt what God has said. Don't be fooled by his cunning tactics! He first checks if you know what God has said. Once the Enemy knows that you have not a clue about what God has said, he then goes to the next step to defeat you by removing the idea of a penalty or pain from the disobedience that you would commit against God. But if you decide that an action will be painful, then you will not be likely to commit that action.

Every time God gives a warning, He follows our disobedience with a penalty and pain. Every time we sin something dies. Satan tries to entice us by making temptations seem harmless and even beneficial. That thought of benefit gave Eve what seemed to be a sense of power. The power that was given to her already was through her submission to God through her husband. Adam's sense of power was going to come through his obedience to God and his obedience to God's Word. The Enemy did his damage by saying *"ye shall not surely die."* In other words, you won't die literally. That seemingly removed the penalty and pain from any disobedience. Let's look at the next thought planted. Genesis 3:5 says, *"For God doth know that in the day ye eat thereof, then your eyes shall be opened, and ye shall be as gods, knowing good and evil."* Not only does this seem logical, it also seems like a benefit. Why does the statement seem logical? God had already said, *"Let us make man in our image and after our likeness."*

But this was actually a step down from what God had said. The reason was Satan said **as gods** (lower case) but God said **in our likeness** (upper case). What God said put them in a class equal to his class, but what Satan said put them in a class equal to his class. Philippians 2:5-6 says, *"Let this mind be in you, which was also in Christ Jesus: Who, being in the form of God, thought it not robbery to be equal with God."* Satan's class is always lower. Not only is Satan's class lower, he will never share equally with anyone. The reason God said that they would die was that they were created like God Himself and if they sinned they would no longer live as God lived—that they would die out of the sphere of God's existence.

There is a great danger in our seeing and desiring what is outside our sphere of godly authority. God has given us power and authority in the realm where He has planted us. If you get talked into something that God has not called you into, you will move out of where God placed you. You must stay where God has planted you. Next we will look at some things that get us out of the realm of God's existence.

Step 4. Change Your Environment

There are things that you are accustomed to having around, but this is a time of change. God has called us into another environment where we are not accustomed to the things that are around us. If we've been drinkers, then we must change that drinking environment. This is an area where we must be honest with ourselves. What can we change that we may not want to change? Remember that without changing the things that are around you, you will bring the same addiction into your new area. Jesus said in Matthew 9:17, *"Neither do men put new wine into old bottles: else the bottles break..."* Likewise I say to you, "Don't put old, decayed things in new places lest it take away from the new place." There are people whom you can't be around anymore because they will draw you back into old things. Some of you may work with, attend church with, or even live in the same location as those whom you should not be around, and you may ask the question, "What if I can't get away from them?" This may be a very interesting place to be. If that is the case, you have to do the same thing that the previous person had to do. Make a quality decision that you will have limited dealings with them as much as possible. If God has allowed you to be in that kind of a situation, then please know that God has also given you the grace in your quality decision to endure the test. Take hold of this scripture:

"There hath no temptation taken you but such as is common to man: but God is faithful, who will not suffer you to be tempted above that ye are able; but will with the temptation also make a way to escape, that ye may be able to bear it." (1 Cor. 10:13)

Anytime you find yourself in that kind of situation, know that God is there with you. He stated in the Word that He would never leave you nor forsake you. God is faithful and will provide for us adequate grace to overcome every temptation. If God promises us that He will not allow us to be tempted above that which we can bear and provides a way to escape, then you can believe it and hold Him to that promise. You can take it to the bank! When change comes, things change. You never go into new places with the old stuff that kept you bound in the old place.

If you are dealing with relationships, what can you honestly change without stepping out of God's will in terms of your purpose? There are times in relationships when you simply cannot change everything that is around you. The will of God then takes precedence over your just running out of a place. You may have to back up from some things, change some conditions of the relationship, and make a quality decision on what things must be. But by all means, stay in the will of God.

The safest place to be in all of the earth is in the will of God. God can keep you anywhere as long as you are determined to stay in His will. Many tests are intended to get you out of your place of purpose and away from your person of purpose, so that you do not hear the Word that will launch you into God's purpose.

Making and Standing on Your Quality Decision

My former pastor used to say all the time, "If you don't stand for something you will fall for anything." I realized long ago that my success in anything that I would do would come only if I made quality decisions that I was willing to stand on. Therefore, I had to decide to get away from people who could not help me and others who did not mean me well. Did I love these people? Yes, of course I did! But the fact that I loved them did not mean that I had to stay around them. They did not have a piece of the puzzle that fit into my life that would launch me toward my destiny.

Make the Will of God First Place in Your Decision

What can we do to help make quality decisions? Outside of God's will nothing else really matters. God's will has to be first place in your life. We must also become purpose-driven in our decisions. For every decision that you make, ask yourself, "Why am I deciding to do this?" If your reason is not one of purpose, then don't do it. You should not go to places where you don't belong if they are not part of your purpose. What do I mean by purpose-driven? The decisions that you are making should grow you, mature you, and build your faith. What change will come about as a result of your decision? Are you going just to be going? That reason has no purpose behind it.

Remember, God is a God of purpose, a God of design, a God of planning, and a God of objectivity. God has a purpose in mind for everything He does. If we are going to be the people of God, then we need to operate on the same principles so that we can get the same results. **If you are getting bad results from your decisions, then there is a strong possibility that your decisions are not based on godly principles. Decisions based on God's Word enable you to stand and demand the God kind of results. When you hold onto God's Word, favor comes upon you to accomplish what you are after.**

Evaluate Those Around You
Ask yourself the following questions when evaluating folks around you. What purpose do they serve in your life? Do they have your problem or your answer? If they have your problem, then don't stay around them. What has God said to you regarding the person who has the same problem as yours? Your answer may help you to determine whether to keep them around. It is possible to let in the wrong people if their presence will not help launch you into the blessing. Please understand that we are not referring to your spouse. If that is what your spouse represents, then counseling or pastoral direction is needed. There has to be a way to work that out.

Remember Lot and Abram? The Lord said unto Abram in Genesis 12:1, *"Get thee out of thy country, and from thy kindred, and from thy father's house, unto a land that I will shew thee."* Abram disobeyed one detail that God had given him. He was to separate himself from his kindred and he didn't. He took Lot! We need to obey all that God is saying. Abram's disobedience caused him trouble that could have been avoided. There arose a fight between the servants of Lot and the servants of Abram. Leaving some people behind may eliminate the problems that we are having.

Disconnect from the problem

Disconnect from the problem that seems to hold you from your goal. You have to determine who and what things prevent you from reaching your destination. Once you identify the problem, disconnect if possible! Abram had to send Lot in the direction that he chose. Then Abram went in the direction that Lot did not choose. Lot took the land that seemed to be more prosperous. Isn't it amazing how God prospered Abram in a seemingly barren land? God also changed the name of Abram to Abraham. When you make the decision to correct things and obey God, He always comes through in a way that is prosperous. If God will ever prosper you in a way that you may desire, you must get away from people who don't want to be blessed. The word "connection" carries the basic connotation of union, link, or bond. Whenever you have such close relationship, it is almost always affected, infected, hindered, or blessed by those you are in relationship with. The choice is yours; what will you do?

Step 5. Maintaining Correct Boundaries

Many times we do not set up proper boundaries for protection. Many believers even feel guilty for having boundaries in place. We often question when it is appropriate to have limits or borders. We normally ask such great questions as:

• Can I set boundaries and still be compassionate toward people?

• What are correct boundaries since I am a Christian?

• What if people become offended by the boundaries I set?

• What do I say to those who want time, money, or love from me?

• Why do I get this feeling of being wrong while setting boundaries?

• Am I being ungodly and selfish when I set these kinds of parameters around me?

Why do I have the feeling of wanting to control other people when I don't get my way? In owning real estate we will go at length to set boundaries around our properties to discourage intruders. We will even build a garage to protect our cars from the children playing in our neighborhood. Why do we feel that way?

It is a matter of protecting ourselves and the things that rightfully belong to us. We set up mailboxes to receive mail, ensuring that our address is visible for the postman so that our mail is not delivered to our neighbor's house. Why? There is a sense of ownership of the mail that is addressed to you. The inability to establish appropriate boundaries at appropriate times and with appropriate people has proven to be very destructive. Let's get onto a healthier road toward healthy boundaries that will bring about healthy relationships to develop healthy homes.

Establish a boundary and stick with it. You will find that when you create boundaries for the people who surround you and enforce them, the people will often yield and adhere to them. Even your children can become accustomed to sticking with your boundaries when you set them in place and enforce them. Your children will invariably test you to find out if and how they can weaken your boundaries. They could use such tactics as gifts, the spouse, sweet talk, a fit of tantrums, or crying to weaken the boundaries. Some have been successful in doing so! **Stand firm!**

Why are you able to maintain your boundaries? We often have to treat the breaking of boundaries as if it is sin. When we sin, it is clear that pain or consequences are attached to the sin. If we treat our boundaries the same way, then people are more likely to submit to the boundaries. **Don't deviate from the stand that you take!** Be totally determined. Send the message, **"Do not cross this line that I have drawn."** Learning to say "no" is the key to being boundary-successful. **Don't worry about what others may think.** You may have been offered drugs, homosexuality, lesbianism, or even a chance at robbing the corner store, but your wise answer was "no." Some of us may have to admit that we said "yes" to some of those unwise decisions and that it was the very one that you craved one point. You must find and take another approach to your craving! Think of the price that you may have to pay in yielding to that desire! **What hinders you from keeping your boundaries strong? Know this: Incorrect desires are opposed to correct boundaries.**

Step 6. Steps of Digression Out of the Presence Of God

When someone sins, the person always steps away from the presence of God. Sin and addiction will lead you out of the presence of God and into the presence of the Enemy. You will always be in either one or the other's presence. Let's look at some of the steps of digression.

Digression Step # 1—Eve saw
Something Eve saw got her attention. It is imperative that we stay focused and not take our attention off what God has already said. The very trick of the Devil is to move your attention from whatever God has already indicated. The Devil can never take you some place that you can't see with your inner eye, or with your heart. You must protect your heart if you are to walk in the Spirit. Remember what God said

regarding those who were building the tower of Babel? David said whatever they imagined to do they would be able to do because they were one. Anytime God gives you a thing to do the only way you can do it is to become one with Him. That was the reason the Devil had to get Eve to see his way. By doing so she was able to convince Adam to see the same way. The ultimate outcome of that decision was that they would become one with Satan. Remember, God's system of operation is agreement. If you agree with Satan, then you will have his results. If you agree with God in whatever He says or desires to do, then you will have whatever He said that you would have regardless of how farfetched it may sound.

Adam and the woman started in total oneness with God, but that total oneness ended when they both saw outside of God. Their level of safety was in seeing what God saw. They never knew that they were naked until they saw outside themselves and moved into the realm that Satan was locked into. Remember, God said that if they partook of the forbidden fruit, they would die. The word "die" means to "cease living, become senseless," which meant that they became every bit of that after they were partakers of the forbidden fruit. The proof of that can be found in the statement, "They hid themselves from the presence of the Lord." You cannot be created in the presence of God, then want to hide from His presence and say that you have not died out of His presence. You have to be prayerful about what you go after because it may look good to the eye but kill you spiritually. There are things to remember when you go off into the sight realm. What you see causes things in you to be awakened. It looks good to partake of; it looks pleasant to the eyes; and it creates unwarranted, uncontrollable, and unnatural desire. All of those kinds of things begin to happen when you start to see outside of the realm where God has placed you.

Digression Step # 2—Eve took

Eve's purpose as a woman was never to take, and as with any other woman it is to receive, not to take or give; yet Eve did both. When the Enemy got her to see and created desire in her, he got her focus off so that she did not see clearly into her purpose. Once people get off in their purpose, they will also get off in their direction. The only way that the Devil could get Adam off in his direction was to affect his weakest link. Adam's weakest link was Eve. Therefore, in order to get Adam's focus off, the Enemy had to get Eve's focus off.

It is imperative that we protect our weakest link. Many times we get so focused in ourselves that we forget about our weakest link. If your wife is your weakest link, then remember that you will never be able to go anywhere without her, and fulfilling your destiny will be determined by whether or not you strengthen her. You very well could be left open and vulnerable because your weakest link could not cover you. To protect yourself from addiction and vulnerability, you must strengthen your weakest link. Eve was greatly affected by what she saw. Therefore Adam's responsibility was to work with her in the area of her being focused. I think after hearing this you could appreciate the scripture that says, "Prefer others above yourself." If you prefer someone else before yourself, then he or she may very well be the one who will end up saving you from vulnerability.

If you are in ministry, it is to your advantage to keep those who serve you strong because they may well be the ones who will protect you from the things that would captivate you in your state of being vulnerable. Eve was not properly instructed and was not able to protect her husband. Why do I say that? Because Eve did not know exactly what God said. Adam did not clearly instruct Eve on what God clearly instructed him to do.

Digression Step # 3—Eve did eat

It wasn't what Eve ate that was wrong but her disobedience. So many times we get caught up on the wrong things. For instance, God once said to me, **"Rodney, I never send people to hell because they sinned. People go to hell for rejecting me."** We get caught majoring on trying not to sin instead of majoring on being sure that we don't reject Jesus. It is much easier not to reject Jesus than it is to try not to sin. Had Eve devoted her time toward being conscious of never rejecting God and faithfully following His instructions, she would not have placed herself in that situation. It is only a matter of what your focus is that makes the difference between easy and hard. That is an amazing revelation that we all need to understand. Do we try not to fornicate, commit adultery, lie, and steal, or do we fall so deeply in love with Jesus that we just honor Him in our body? I think the easiest thing to do is just to fall deeply in love with Jesus so that we will not sin against Him, will honor Him with our body, and will honor Him in our lifestyle.

One of the reasons we stay in addictions is that in our attempt to break them we shoot at the wrong things. Let's take a look at some of the things that we need to aim at if we are to hit the desired target. The number one key that must be remembered is to go after the root problem (cause) not the surface problem (effect).

Drug or Alcohol Addiction—Is there something in your life that you are trying to escape? Did it start as a teen or as an adult? There is something that you are trying to escape, run from, vacate, and not deal with. Most people who are in that kind of situation don't like who they are, and the norm is always to do something that will make themselves different. When you are trying to abandon your position of how you see yourself and identify with the position of someone else, we call that cause the missing identity.

Sexual Sin Addiction—The cause of sexual sin addiction is lack of validation. The one who should have validated that person did not. The effect of that is the person is now left in a posture of vulnerability. Somewhere in that person's past, he or she felt damaged in femininity or masculinity and must now prove self-worth in a certain area of personal manhood or womanhood. The person who battles in this area of life is locked into an addiction, sometimes for life, to prove self-worthiness. The root cause in that situation is not sex but worth. If that person could build up self-worth, then the seeming problem in the area of sex would disappear. Somewhere in this person's life he or she was made to feel inadequate in performance. People who excessively pursue the opposite sex and somewhere in their past have been damaged by a person of the opposite sex tend to have difficulty in starting new relationships with the opposite sex. Therefore, they run after whomever they can get just to prove to themselves that they can get someone of the opposite sex. The problem with that is they run after many and can never satisfy the flesh.

Spending Addiction—We must look at the past of people with spending addictions. Somewhere in their past they formed a special escape from an area in their life where they have been damaged by someone or by people in their life. The only thing about this group is that their outer man has been criticized to the point where they can never get comfortable about their appearance. Yet their damage is still internal. If we could ever get this kind of person healed of the internal damage that was done, then we could get spending under control. Think about that: there is not one thing wrong with spending, but when a person has been damaged within, that person would resort to spending as an escape. Therefore, the addictive behavior would be spending, but that is not the real problem. Yet we are more likely to attack them in the area of their spending, but that is only the effect of that cause. That is not the cause itself. Let's learn to attack the root and not damage the person.

Digression Step # 4—Eve gave

One of the most important things that a man and a woman can learn is that the woman was never made to be the giver in the relationship. The man is the giver, and if he ever allows that order to get displaced, then the family structure will get out of place. When Eve became the giver, that was the major break in that family unit. When you think of the way God made the body of man you know that he was made to be the giver. That thought could only cause you to think of how the woman's body is made, which then brings us to know that she certainly must be the receiver. Everything that is given to the woman is reproduced. God made the woman with like purpose as the ground, which receives and then multiplies what it receives. Because the woman is so productive, it then becomes almost impossible for her not to spread what she receives. The damage comes if what she spreads is sinful. Because the woman has a spreading or multiplying ability after she has received, she is most likely to be the one who will wrestle with the spirit of gossip. The bad thing about that time of Eve's multiplication was that it was going to affect not just Adam but also the whole world and those who were to come. The cause was that she ate what was forbidden; the effect was that he ate, too. When Adam ate what forbidden, that action started a generational effect in all that came after him. The generational effect of our sin does not start addiction but does start an appetite for things that we have never tapped into ourselves.

Bishop R. S. Walker

Chapter 4

Poison That Penetrates Our Youth

Raising a Standard

God has been speaking to the body of Christ for a while about raising a standard. One area in which we must raise that standard is music. We, as saved folks and as adults, at times get caught up with our eyes closed, revering, flowing in the moment of Christian music, singing "Hallelujah!" not realizing that over in the corner our children are listening to some other kind of music. And believe me, it is a message of worship, except it's not worshipping the Great God our Jehovah. One of the reasons that they listen to things like that is that they don't understand how detrimental it is to their lives.

So they brought the ark of God, and set it in the midst of the tent that David had pitched for it: and they offered burnt sacrifices and peace offerings before God. And when David had made an end of offering the burnt offerings and the peace offerings, he blessed the people in the name of the LORD. And he dealt to every one of Israel, both man and woman, to every one a loaf of bread, and a good piece of flesh, and a flagon of wine. And he appointed certain of the Levites to minister before the ark of the LORD, and to record, and to thank and praise the LORD God of Israel: Asaph

78

the chief, and next to him Zechariah, Jeiel, and Shemiramoth, and Jehiel, and Mattithiah, and Eliab, and Benaiah, and Obededom: and Jeiel with psalteries and with harps; but Asaph made a sound with cymbals; Benaiah also and Jahaziel the priests with trumpets continually before the ark of the covenant of God. Then on that day David delivered first this psalm to thank the LORD into the hand of Asaph and his brethren. Give thanks unto the LORD, call upon his name, make known his deeds among the people. Sing unto him, sing psalms unto him, talk ye of all his wondrous works. Glory ye in his holy name: let the heart of them rejoice that seek the LORD. Seek the LORD and his strength, seek his face continually. Remember his marvelous works that he hath done, his wonders, and the judgments of his mouth; O ye seed of Israel his servant, ye children of Jacob, his chosen ones. He is the LORD our God; his judgments are in all the earth. Be ye mindful always of his covenant; the word which he commanded to a thousand generations. (1 Chron. 16:1-15)

Youth will come from all over and flood the altar with all of their CDs, their ungodly posters, and different things like that. I believe they are going to cast them on the altar, as it was done in the Book of Acts, when they brought all their art and cast it into the fire. I believe we will have that same kind of experience. Instead of our taking this stuff and just burning it, we need to cast it on the altar and believe God for the salvation of every one of those authors. We need to put a demand on God to save every one of those singers' lives. We are hoping that they will come to Levitical priesthood. That may not mean a whole lot to some of you. Let's just talk about who really should be singing.

Let me talk to the people who sing and ask why God selected you. Sometimes the divine purpose of certain things on earth becomes defiled. Think about the blessing that can come from listening to music or the purpose for which it was actually created and the damage that it can do if it is not centered around God and His purpose. Anytime we change something from its God-intended use, it becomes perverted and then functions opposite of God's original intent. We must attempt to come back to the truth of the Word. The reason we are not dealing with our struggles is that we have not changed what goes into our ear gate. Some people might be struggling with fornication, adultery, lying, or producing illegitimate babies. These issues can be changed based on what is going into your ear.

Do you realize that music can do major damage in your life if it's not centered around what God wants? Please understand that I am not saying music has to be sad and dreary; not all gospel music is sad and dreary. I thank God for songs like "Amazing Grace" that cause us to reach back in history for what music is really all about. I appreciate what God is doing through artists whose songs have a specific purpose in the kingdom. We can go even deeper into contemporary types of music. However, when music starts to take on a form that God has not dealt with, it begins to get into our spirit man and causes us to do things that we really don't want to do. Here are seven questions that I propose to you:

1. What is the purpose of music and those who sing it?
2. Is the wrong music harmful and why?
3. How can music bless the life of someone?
4. Why shouldn't we listen to all music?
5. Should we listen to a CD that has one gospel song on it?
6. Can we listen to secular music and still serve God?
7. What can we listen to?

Tell us, what music can we listen to that will be acceptable to God? Now, this is the frustration that we really have to address. What can we do? Some of us came from a church full of adults, and it was all about adults. Anytime you are consistently telling somebody what not to do, guess what they are going to do. Why? Because there is a "duplicator" that's down on the inside of every individual. Let us really think about this and effectively deal with our children accordingly. You tell them not to do a thing, and they go out and do what you say not to do. Now, here is the point I'm really trying to get across to you. Ask yourself, Am I really demonstrating for them what not to do? What's going to stand stronger in their mind is what they see you do, not what they hear you say to do.

The Power of Words

Let's go a little further. Consider the effect of words, because before we can even deal with any of this, I have to tell you about how words affect you.

It is the spirit that quickeneth; the flesh profiteth nothing: the words that I speak unto you, they are spirit, and they are life. (John 6:63 KJV)

So here's the question: Why would we do things that we really don't want to do? Or why do we crave a particular thing? The Devil has to get some words in you. Your parents or somebody saved is standing in the gap for you. The only way the Enemy can get around the prayer wall that your parents built up is to get you on the opposite side of that wall, so the words will not be deposited in you.

Young people, why do you think that some of these little guys come along and start speaking seemingly all the right stuff on the inside of you? They know what you want to hear. They may say something like, "Girl, you are all that and a bag of chips." Now, see, they begin to speak all this stuff on the inside of you until you begin to speak and behave the same way.

And he said unto them, Take heed what ye hear: with what measure ye mete, it shall be measured to you: and unto you that hear shall more be given. (Mark 4:24)

The very words that you hear, the songs that you are listening to, are going in your spirit man. And remember the Devil knows the Bible, which means the

Devil can get you to hear the words to the song. He wants to paint an image in your spirit when you hear what the young boy or young girl is saying and what the man or the woman is saying. Then he can start adding more to you based on what he wants to get to you.

Take heed what ye hear: with what measure ye mete, it shall be measured to you: and unto you that hear shall more be given.

Take heed therefore how ye hear: for whosoever hath, to him shall be given; and whosoever hath not, from him shall be taken even that which he seemeth to have. (Luke 8:18)

Jesus is saying, "If I could just get you to hear the way I really need you to hear, I could get anything to you." So what does the Devil do? The Devil counterfeits that and says, "If I can get them to hear anything, then I can get more of what I want to them.

Do you ever wonder why guys walk up to the ladies and present them with all kinds of opportunity? And sometimes it looks as if they come out from nowhere. The Devil will say something to you to destroy your destiny. The Devil wants to stop you, so don't let the Devil stop you. Grab hold of the Word of God. The only way to really do this is to quiet the Devil when he speaks to you. The Devil is not only showing up on the scene. He's got to make it attractive. The Devil already understands that the person has no Christian parents, so the person needs to create a sound. We need to create a sound and put Jesus or God in it.

Let's go over to the Book of James and remember every single thing that you hear goes into your ear gate. And then once it goes through your ear gate and you have actually heard it, then it begins to be processed. That is why we have to watch what we actually listen to. The Book of James tells us about this process.

Have you ever really asked yourself, "How did I get here? I'm in a spot right now and I don't know how I got here. I'm just messed up right now. How did I get here? How did I even get into this situation?" There are folks in prison right now just wondering, "How did I get here? I mean, what was the process of my getting to this place? How did it happen to me? Or how did it happen again?" Look, here is the thing—watch what you are hearing. Remember, once it goes through your ear gate it has to go through a particular process. Once it goes through that process, the results are where you find yourself.

Let no man say when he is tempted, I am tempted of God: for God cannot be tempted with evil, neither tempteth he any man: But every man is tempted, when he is drawn away of his own lust, and enticed. Then when lust hath conceived, it bringeth forth sin: and sin, when it is finished, bringeth forth death. (James 1:13-15)

Remember every man is tempted; yes, every one of us gets tempted. When he is drawn away of his own lust, however, don't make the word "lust" a bad word all the time. The word "lust" merely means desire. But every man is tempted when he is drawn away because of his own lust or his own desire.

Words Form a Picture

When lust has been conceived or when the desire has entered and taken form, that is when you go after what was conceived. A man is enticed once he sees a picture of something he desires. More than likely women are enticed when they hear the right stuff. For instance, only women will say, "Child, did you hear his voice on the phone?" A man may say, "She sure sounds sexy, but I wonder what she looks like." The man wants to see the woman who is attached to the voice.

Once the word has gotten on the inside, it creates an appetite, and then your emotions are totally involved. How do you stop your emotions from taking your body somewhere it should not be? This is done by stopping the words. When people talk to you inappropriately or incorrectly, if it's not consistent with the Word of God, stop them immediately. This will stop your senses from reacting to the spoken words. And guess what? The Devil already knows that you are not going to let Brother Billy Bob in the house. He knows that you are not going to let Susan Jane anywhere near you. So here's what the Enemy does. He sends the words directly to you in the form of a record, CD, or tape. As you are sitting back listening, you start to think about Billy Bob or Susan Jane, and before you realize, you have been enticed with another opportunity. Look, the Devil is slick, slimy, and tricky. The Bible says that every person is tempted when he is drawn away with his own lust or enticed. The Devil is not satisfied unless he can get you drawn away. How do you get drawn away? When words are formed, a picture is painted in your mind, and then you follow the picture.

Perverted Music

Singers are always anointed and appointed, regardless of what they have chosen to sing. Some singers you hear every day, singing vulgar stuff. Guess what? They were anointed to sing, especially the ones who are very effective and popular. But they did not wait on their godly appointment. The Devil appointed them to use what God gave to them and blinded them as believers to pervert you. What does it mean to be "perverted"? It means to distort or to operate outside of its natural use. Be mindful always that you have been purposed of God to bring Him glory and to give Him praise.

As singers are appointed to sing, they always represent the spirit of that song. Anything you constantly listening to you will eventually sing. You become a representative of that song. How would you like to be a representative of a song that is sung by an artist whose message is against God's will? Some of you already represent it. Do you know why? Because you heard it and it became a part of your spirit, and then you acted it out. You do not know why you act as provocatively as you do. Some of you don't know why you dress as provocatively as you dress. There are a few things that music is designed to do.

And he appointed certain of the Levites to minister before the ark of the LORD, and to record, and to thank and praise the LORD God of Israel…(1 Chron. 16:4)

According to 1 Chronicles 16, there are particular things that God expects music to do. First, we find music being used by appointed representatives of God. Whom are you ultimately representing when you listen to recording artists whose negative, demeaning messages are against God's will? You are representing the Devil himself through their music.

Second, another purpose of music is to praise the Lord. What God or god are you praising when you are listening to the music you like? Do you understand?

Third, music is to talk about His wonderful works. Can you just think about recording artists whose messages are against God's will? Their messages are not about God's wonderful works. They bring so much glory to Satan. Take your religious hat off. We need to change some of the radio stations. Do we want to do those things that give honor to Satan and the spirit of death? Or are we really challenged to bring glory and honor to Jesus Christ? We have been designed, appointed, and anointed to bring glory and honor to God.

But I will sing of thy power; yea, I will sing aloud of thy mercy in the morning: for thou hast been my defence and refuge in the day of my trouble. Unto thee, O my strength, will I sing: for

God is my defence, and the God of my mercy. (Ps. 59:16-17)

Sing forth the honour of his name: make his praise glorious. (Ps. 66:2)

"You hungry and tired, you give me food and let me sleep, I come to you weak, and you give me strength not deep. You call me a sheep, you lead me to green pastures only after that I keep the focus in between the chapters you give me the word and only accent I interpret. Lord, why is it I go through so much pain?"

What we are actually hearing is a man that God is pulling on. God is pulling on this man, and he put on the CD what God is saying to him. Then he wants to project it as if he got a word from the Lord. Do you understand what I am saying? So then in his next breath what does he talk about? In the very next breath, he says, "I don't give a hell about y'all niggas, because you ain't gave me nothing." So then we wonder why our children do not care. That's what our children are listening to while we are going Hallelujah! We have our eyes closed. We need to open up our eyes. Thank God for the Hallelujah, we need that, but then when we leave the house and shut the door, the music changes. This is happening in your house, where you pay the bills. Let's expose the Devil so we will know what's going into the ears of our children. Who do you think is getting glory from this? Is glory going to God?

The artist of the lyrics above continued in the song to talk about heaven. He says in his lyrics, "If I have to receive pain take care of my boy that just died." We need to be able to effectively converse with our children and the children in the neighborhood.

A man's belly shall be satisfied with the fruit of his mouth; and with the increase of his lips shall he be filled. Death and life are in the power of the tongue: and they that love it shall eat the fruit thereof. (Prov. 18:20-21)

Music is purposed to bring glory to God, and to edify, build up, and stimulate faith in us. I really don't think this kind of music is doing that. This may seem like a bit much, but this is not even the beginning of what's out there.

Is the wrong music harmful, and if so, why?

The very things that proceed out of your mouth will be the things that you reap in life. **You become what you listen to and receive in life the things you say or sing.** Death and life are in the power of the tongue and much of what you're receiving is what you have declared in word or song.

What are our children becoming based on what they are hearing?

Why do our children dress and act provocatively? Could recording artists who sing negative messages have anything to do with that? Remember, **words are spirit and they are life.** If we wonder why there seems to be a spirit of lust that lingers around our children, wonder no more. Let recording artists who sing negative messages tell you. This is very vulgar, but what our children listen to seems to frame their thinking because we are not doing what the Book of Proverbs says, *"Train up a child in the way he should go and when he is old he will not depart from it." The next verse says; "Whosoever findeth a wife findeth a good thing, and obtaineth favour of the LORD."*

And we sometimes wonder, why is the Lord not sending the man or the woman that we desire? We have some things we have to get in order.

Train Up a Child

Speaking of training up a child in the way he should go, who is mentoring your child, or even your stepchildren and youth relatives that God expects you to raise? How about recording artists who send negative, disrespectful, soul-damaging messages to our youth? Even the way they conduct their lives sets a poor example. Then they influence the children in their families, who mimic them and then record their own seemingly harmless music. These children have the ability to influence your child the same way they are being mentored. When we allow our children to listen to these recording artists, we are giving the okay in many areas for them to be free to do things that we never approve.

Yea, and all that will live godly in Christ Jesus shall suffer persecution. But evil men and seducers

shall wax worse and worse, deceiving, and being deceived. But continue thou in the things which thou hast learned and hast been assured of, knowing of whom thou hast learned them; And that from a child thou hast known the holy scriptures, which are able to make thee wise unto salvation through faith which is in Christ Jesus. All scripture is given by inspiration of God, and is profitable for doctrine, for reproof, for correction, for instruction in righteousness: That the man of God may be perfect, thoroughly furnished unto all good works. (2 Tim. 3:12-17)

Should We Listen to a CD That Has One Gospel Song on It?

Beloved, believe not every spirit, but try the spirits whether they are of God: because many false prophets are gone out into the world. Hereby know ye the Spirit of God: Every spirit that confesseth that Jesus Christ is come in the flesh is of God: And every spirit that confesseth not that Jesus Christ is come in the flesh is not of God: and this is that spirit of antichrist, whereof ye have heard that it should come; and even now already is it in the world. Ye are of God, little children, and have overcome them: because greater is he that is in you, than he that is in the world. They are of the world: therefore speak they of the world, and the world heareth them. We are of God: he that knoweth God heareth us; he that is not of God heareth not us. Hereby know we the spirit of truth,

and the spirit of error. (1 John 4:1-6)

We have already heard some songs that had a form of gospel but were not gospel at all. Those in the music industry **know that there are lukewarm Christians** who think that all they need is a form of what appears to be gospel and they will be one of the first to buy it. One female recording artist had to say some things about what she called a "former Deacon" she had in her web and one who could not get away, no doubt. **How would this affect us or our children? Things such as this will cause a craving on the inside and will also open a door for the Devil to come in your life.**

Another recording artist deals with his picture of heaven that is far from the truth. This says to our children it's all right to do what you want and you'll still go to heaven. In a song called "Heaven," the thought of what he said brings me to understand 2 Timothy 3:1-7:

This know also, that in the last days perilous times shall come. For men shall be lovers of their own selves, covetous, boasters, proud, blasphemers, disobedient to parents, unthankful, unholy, Without natural affection, trucebreakers, false accusers, incontinent, fierce, despisers of those that are good, Traitors, heady, high-minded, lovers of pleasures more than lovers of God; Having a form of godliness, but denying the power thereof: from such turn away. For of this sort are they which creep into houses, and lead

captive silly women laden with sins, led away with divers lusts, Ever learning, and never able to come to the knowledge of the truth.

Can We Listen to Regular Music and Still Serve God?

We certainly could listen to regular music, but it would be difficult to serve God in purity and holiness. That really means that there would be heartbreaks, disappointments, abuse, and many other things like that. The wrong music sets the pace for you to have desire for the wrong type of men or women. What gets into your life or stays out is up to you. **The time has come to set our standards high.** The choice is yours and mine. Some recording artists say things that set up our young ladies for heartbreak. The way the Enemy sets you up through music is by making you feel that it is all right for you to be picked up (booked) only to be let down. One recording artist sings, "How can it be just us two? I never loved you. We just met and I just f... you." This is the way you are viewed when you don't keep your standards high. You give up the goods and you are viewed as cheap trash or B's that come or go.

What God Says About You

God says you are fearfully and wonderfully made. God say your price is far above rubies. God further says that you are a royal priesthood, a holy nation, and a peculiar people. He says that you should show forth the praise of Him who has brought you out of darkness and placed you in His marvelous light.

Death and Life are in the Power of the Tongue

Why is the wrong music harmful? Words coming out of our mouths start to form things. Whether it comes out of our mouths in song or in words, music forms things. You become what you listen to and receive in life the things you say or think.

We already dealt with the question about why we dress so provocatively. Let's take a look at female recording artists who dress provocatively. This is who our children are listening to and watching. Look at these artists—they have cute faces, though they might have gotten a little messed up trying to make some corrections. They look like this so they can attract each and every one. They have just the right voices so they won't leave out the women, and they have just enough hate for men so that they can really grab hold of the women who really don't like men anyway. Our kids are becoming what they hear. It took me days to get this. Do you know why? Because I had to stop and go into prayer and start building myself back up. Why? Because of the vulgar mess of what these recording artists are saying—you have to build yourself up. I'm saved, sanctified, Holy Ghost filled, and baptized.

This is the point that I'm trying to make. Our children feel this way day by day when listening to this music, but they don't know what they are feeling is wrong. I'm not talking about the feeling to fornicate.

I'm saying that when you know that the very presence of God is in you, and then you hear and see stuff like this, it attacks God's presence. And when you feel the presence being attacked, then you go off speaking in tongues. Oh, it makes you want to pray.

Let me tell you something: some of you saved folks have your head sticking in the gospel sand and and you do not realize your children are going to hell. So we have to raise a standard and say, "As for me and my house, we will serve the Lord." My children aren't going to hell. We have to correct what our children are listening to and doing. If we don't correct what they are listening to, there is no way we will be able to correct what they are doing. Please understand this: if your children want to go out and mess around like these recording artists are talking about, they're going to do it. But you can correct what they are hearing and put another desire inside of them. Don't beat them with the Bible. They need to see or feel a particular way and watch our lives.

Who is Mentoring You?

Let's talk about who has become a mentor to our children. What about recording artists and the children who copy them and become junior recording artists? We already know what the children will become based on the adult mentor's life. One recording artist child says he's taking "little" out of his recording name because he's no longer a child. All we're doing is fixing up our children to be able to say, "Don't call me the little baby name that you call me because I am not a child anymore."

Music ministry is supposed to be a vehicle that will enhance every single thing that God wanted to do on the earth. The Levites in 1 Chronicles 16 would be what we would recognize today as a deacon or your music ministers, the choir members, the praise and worship members. They were appointed in order to represent God in music ministry on the earth. I didn't say in the church. Let me say that one more time because a lot of you will miss this, because see this is what we do—we separate those that are assigned to bring in music into the world, and then we recognize those who will bring in music in the church, and we make the two separate. God never intended for them to be separate. See, no one sang unless God appointed him or her. Nobody just decided to form a community choir. For example, you decide to form a community choir because you can't get along with the folks in the church. And we don't really want to be under authority. And see, everyone must be under someone's authority. Most community choirs are a whole bunch of different folks not under anyone's authority. Then you ask, "Well, what church are you from?" Then they answer, "I'm from such-and-such church," and "I'm from the other church." Some may answer, "As a matter of fact, I don't even go to church." And so you have all these different voices that are thrown together to make up the community choir, and no one's under authority to anyone.

But now in the beginning when God created music, God appointed them to sing. The first reason was to represent Him and carry out music ministry on the earth, as it would please Him. The second reason was to praise the Lord, to bring praise on the earth. Praise does something unique. Praise, the Bible says, steals the avenger, so anytime an enemy rises up, praise stops that enemy. We make the mistake when trouble arises of stopping our singing. But God tells us to sing louder because praise steals the avenger; it stops the Enemy in his tracks. Now we understand the purpose for which God really created music—to stop the Enemy. So anytime you have music that starts trouble, now we know where that music originated. Now I didn't say music that is controversial. I said music that starts trouble, music that draws demonic forces from particular places and begins to open up doors that we don't want to open. The third reason that God created music was to declare His wonderful works. Isn't it amazing that we come up with things like, "I'm climbing up the rough side of the mountain"? Then tell me how that articulates to a group of believers the wonderful works of God. Going up the rough side—how in the world does that communicate the wonderful works of God? It does not. Therefore, we must be prayerful about what we are singing.

Anything that we sing or say actually creates our world tomorrow. So now I ask you, what have you been creating?

We have all kinds of worldly reasons that we gather for the purpose of music. If we are just looking for a good time with music, we bring that same spirit into the church. If we wanted to celebrate in past times, we got involved with rock. If you were going to a party, you didn't hear blues. You heard rock, soul, and all of that. When you wanted to get your little thing on, then there wasn't any rock. Hello, somebody. Turn the lights down low, baby come close, put your hand in mine, oh, please be kind. Let me touch your heart, let the fire start, oooh, oooh, oooh, oooh. Tell me if it's going to bring about a spirit. Which one is it going to be? A room full of single folks who are going to be provoked? So do you realize a lot of this we bring right in the church? Then you had the group—this is normally the group from the heartbreak hotel; they wanted to sing the sad songs. More than likely if they were men they would listen to blues; if they were women they were listening to the sad songs. You know, I found love on a two-way street and lost it on a lonely highway. I'm sorry a lot of you may not even know what I'm talking about. That's not a song that you're even going to dance to; you're going to sit all the way back in the corner. By this time you're getting really droopy and have lost it on a lonely highway, and by this time you're crying. And you're sitting back thinking about the song and whom you have lost.

Here's the thing that this music doesn't do. It won't create an atmosphere that God can be pleased with nor an atmosphere that God can work in. So as we think about these things, we ask, why do we sing what we sing, and what we are representing? With everything you sing, you're representing somebody or some god. Now which one is it going to be? Let me tell you what you're going to do. You're going to leave this church, you're going to get into your car on this saved parking lot, and you're going to turn on the radio, more than likely. You're going to put on a CD, a tape; you're going to put on something that has to do with music. But when you turn that knob, that's going to speak into your spirit, see, because when you leave church your spirit is wide open, so then the question is, what is it that you're going hear once you leave this place? What are you going to hear? And then what is it going to provoke?

There are particular kinds of music that provoke particular things. I had some individuals who walked up to me after we dealt with some of these recording artists. Sorry, but we dealt with them. I'm not trying to insult your group. And I hope they're not your group any more. What we found out is that you cannot listen to some of them and not be aroused sexually. Why is this? Remember, words are spirit and they are life. So think about when we allow our young people or when we allow ourselves to indulge in that kind of music all day long. And they're going to go to sleep on that. And then they're going to wake up the next day and turn it back on again because they like it. Whatever spirit those words are describing is what the appetite is for what they turn on, inside them. So we have to be educated in this. Like when folks end up in the clubs, and they just call themselves having a good time, the Enemy is programming the next move that he's going to make on them. When the Devil wants to defeat us as believers, he sends people who will talk about doubt and unbelief. He'll allow you to hear it on the radio. A lot of the things we listen to program the next defeat that the Enemy has planned.

Some wonder why they can't stop doing something. It's because the Enemy has already programmed your next defeat. God really wants to do something, but God can't break up your favorite CD and insert some gospel. God needs you to insert the gospel. Please understand that this faith comes by hearing by the Word of God on a consistent basis. You are hearing and hearing and hearing the Word, and the words you hear go into your spirit man. Peace starts to increase for whatever that thing is, even if it's killing. Do you really want to know how the Enemy really got that down on the earth? He programmed it. The more he wanted to defeat you, the more he programmed it into your mind. God desires these things to get into our spirit and stimulate faith.

Someone asked me once, now what about temptation? Okay, now here's the question. Does it stimulate faith? Is it faith-provoking? Does it lift up God? Let's look at it another way. Now I'm talking to you who walk on the line of gospel and rock, or gospel and soul, or gospel and love music. Because every now and then there can't be anything wrong with love music. Hello, there can't be too much wrong with that. Love music, you know, just you and your baby. Can't be too much wrong with that, can there? Well, remember, let's go right back to the principle: words are spirit and they are life. Now what spirit is that? Did you all catch that, what spirit is that? What spirit is behind "My Cheri Amour?" You're the only one my heart beats for. I wish that you were mine. My heart only beats for you and you're not even mine. What! So what spirit is that?

It's going to generate something. I remember that a female recording artist who was popular in the 1970s sang a song in French. Most of us who sang the song didn't even know what she was saying. But the Devil knows French.

A lot of songs have secret messages hidden in them. There is a particular thing the Devil wants to get accomplished, but he can't get it accomplished because there's a hedge built around you. God has you under protective custody so that the Enemy cannot get through to you. So the Enemy has to provoke desire on the inside of you to get you to open up the door. No one can open up the door but you. So what does he do? He allows you to go around some of these unsaved folks.

Praise God, we loved unsaved folks. See, we loved unsaved folks because we used to be there ourselves. We loved unsaved folks because we want to see them saved. God wants us to go down and get them saved, not go down and get on the dance floor with them. You're not going to save them on the dance floor. You're not going to save them looking up at the ceiling. You're not going to save them looking down at the floor. I'm sorry, should I not talk like this? I'm sorry that I have to talk like this. Glory to God! We say this from time to time, look, if they get to milk the cow, why buy it? You let them sit there and milk your cow, whether it's male or female, and then you wonder why they don't marry me, pastor. I'll tell you why—they got the milk. If you got a rascal whether it's a female or male at home living with you and you're not married,

I'll give you a pen and a piece of paper—it's eviction
time. Put him or her out! Why? Because that person is
never going to come into full commitment with you if
he or she gets to milk your cow every time you come
home from church. Say to yourself, sex is fine, but you
need a license. You need a license for that. Folks come
around and they just want to ride.

These are the things you need to be looking for.
Some slickster comes along and wants to date you. I
dare you to ask the brother, "Do you have any
children?" And if he's got one in New York, one in
California, one in Washington, D.C., another in
Pennsylvania, you're next. Particularly if they're two
years apart or less. Don't seek the Lord—you don't
need the Word. I'll give you a word: Run! Are you
catching me here? We need to deal with things like this
because you want to know, "Well, I just need to know
if it is the Lord." You don't need to know that it is the
Lord. Let me tell y'all, leave the brother right there and
say, "I think that this may be the Lord, but I'm going to
leave you right there, and here's what I'm going to do.
I'm going to give you some time. I'm going to let you
prove yourself."

Please hold onto your religious hat if you have one
because my merchandise is good. Come on, I'm in the
Bible, Proverbs 31, if you are a virtuous woman. If you
don't think you're a virtuous woman, then you have no
business getting married anyway, because you need to
know that you are a virtuous woman before you ever
step up to the altar. When you understand that you're a
virtuous woman you can look at yourself in the mirror

and say, "Girl, your merchandise is good." So for anybody who wants the merchandise, there's a license that goes along with the merchandise. Just anybody doesn't qualify. There are prerequisites. There are particular things that apply beforehand that say whether or not you can really have my goods.

See, the problem is that a lot of times young folks and older folks don't really think that they are valuable. And, therefore, they accept whatever comes. Look, I don't care what size you are. You might be a size 1 or a size 100. The real person is inside of that body. And regardless of your size, regardless of your age, regardless of your color, regardless of your nationality, please understand your merchandise is good. It is valuable enough that you just don't give it to everybody. Here's one of the things to remember; I said that the Enemy has a desire to set up and to defeat you. But see, he has to set the stage first. See, he can't come right in and defeat you. If he says he is the Devil and he's come to defeat you, then you're going to go in the opposite direction. But if he comes in a way that really gets your attention, the music sounds just right. There is so much deceit or deception in the message of the music that it ends up setting a stage for you. And you end up defeated by the Enemy.

Consider these young ones that God has given us charge over. I have eight children that I'm responsible for. And then I have all the rest of the children in the church that I'm responsible for. So I don't cut any slack on any of the parents or any of the adults because I'm responsible for those children back there. I didn't bring them into the world, but because they're tied to me I become responsible. One of the reasons we not able to reach our youth today is that we are painting a picture so big and so high for them that they don't ever believe that they could ever reach it. I believe it's time for us to get totally transparent. Let our children know we failed. But let them know they don't have to fail because we failed. We paint an unrealistic picture about like what the Jews did, and Paul rebuked Peter because he was putting some demands on the Gentiles that the Jews were not even living up to. And the Bible says that Paul withstood him to the face. A lot of our children are struggling. They don't know what's going on inside them, not all of them. That's one of the reasons we don't talk about these things. They don't know what's going on. And we don't talk to them. Their hormones are going crazy.

Chapter 5

Generational Curses

A generational curse starts a certain appetite for the family more than it will start an addiction. All addictions start with individuals making a decision themselves. The Bible talks about *"the sin of the fathers coming down on the children to the third and forth generations of them that hated me."* This kind of sin causes an appetite that you may not have chosen yourself. There are times when we may have appetites that are generational, and we have no clue why we desire things. We will also discover some people in the Bible who have some of these kind traits. For instance, Adam brought us all into an appetite for sin that ordinarily we would not have desired. Think about some of the things that you desire to do that you know are incorrect. Where did that appetite for that particular sin come from in your life? This question will be answered as we deal with the subject of generational curses.

Some things need to be fixed before we build and march over into the next season in God. God may be unable to do new things with new people because they may become somewhat contaminated by the old. I'm not saying that anyone is diseased or so troubled that if something new comes around that you'll contaminate it with the old, but it may happen. Sometimes we embrace or hide the old so much that if God did do a new thing, send something or somebody new, we would mess them up with the old stuff. So we have to understand how to separate the old from the new. Then sometimes we have to break up fallow ground and dig around down there to see if there are old roots. We should then pull up those old roots so that when we plant new stuff in the ground, there will come a flow, an anointing, and a fresh breath of God, which will enable us to go into the next place of God.

Jesus went unto the Mount of Olives. And early in the morning he came again into the temple, and all the people came unto him; and he sat down and taught them. And the scribes and Pharisees brought unto him a woman taken in adultery; and when they had set her in the midst, they say unto him, Master, this woman was taken in adultery, in the very act. Now Moses in the law commanded us, that such should be stoned: but what sayest thou? This they said, tempting him, that they might have to accuse him. But Jesus stooped down, and with his finger wrote on the ground, as though he heard them not. So when they continued asking him, he lifted up himself, and said unto them, he that is without sin among you, let him first cast a stone at her. And again he stooped down, and wrote on the ground. And they which heard it, being convicted by their own conscience, went out one by one, beginning at the eldest, even unto the last: and Jesus was left alone, and the woman standing in the midst. When Jesus had lifted up himself, and saw none but the woman, he said unto her, Woman, where are those thine accusers? hath no man condemned thee? She said, No man Lord. And Jesus said unto her, Neither do I condemn thee: go, and sin no more. (John 8:1-11)

Jesus Stooped Down

At this particular point He did not bow; He stooped. There is a difference there. He is saying that I'm not condoning what you did, so I will not bow. But I will stoop and act as if I didn't even hear your accusers. Jesus, in this particular story, did something that was very, very important, and I think that the Pharisees and the scribes did something that a lot of our accusers in this day do. They will get you right out in front of everyone and begin to accuse you. I believe that now is the time when many who have confessed that they are leaders, that they know God, and that they are in the face of God will have their wisdom tried. It wasn't a matter of whether or not Jesus had the right answer here; it was a matter of whether He was going to move according to law or move according to wisdom. Through wisdom, this woman was not condemned by Jesus, but through the law she would have been condemned because of what she did.

Most of us operate in the church as Pharisees and scribes and will not hesitate in bringing condemnation on someone who may truly be wrong. So the Lord allows us to know how to handle particular things. We know people who have truly done something wrong. However, in the process of their being wrong, God never called us to condemn them but to set them free.

When God came into your life and you accepted Him as your Lord and Savior, He gave you the power and authority to expel darkness when you saw it. Every one us will have something that we're going to have to identify and understand.

The Word says that early in the morning Jesus came again into the temple, and all people came unto Him and He sat down and taught them. Let us first picture the setting. All the people have come to the temple and are sitting around Jesus. It is as if they are His students who have gathered around the master. Normally in biblical times, whenever it was a learning time, they taught sitting down.

Now suddenly some Pharisees and scribes walked into the building with this woman who was caught in adultery and in the very act. They abruptly interrupted Jesus. And when they had sat her in their midst, they said to Him, "Master, this woman was taken in adultery, in the very act. Now Moses in the Law commanded us that such should be stoned." You cannot argue with the Word. The second question is, why didn't they go ahead and stone her? You have to watch those who are always bringing something or someone to you with some type of accusations. Why did they not go ahead and stone her? Instead of stoning her, they brought her to Jesus in the company of all of those that respected Him. There was a motive behind this! They knew they had Jesus cornered and that He was going to make the wrong decision. What was Jesus going to say since the law of Moses commanded them to stone a person like this? Many of us are so quick to say, "But what saith

Thou?" They had a problem because Moses had already stated what to do. They wanted to separate Jesus from Moses, not realizing that they were setting this up as if God wanted them to do it.

A distinction had to be made between the old and the new. The Pharisees did not understand what they were really doing. They were saying, "Moses commanded us that such a person should be stoned, but Jesus, you are on this side—we don't want you on our side but on this side, what saith Thou?" This question was not asked with sincerity nor to know His mind but to accuse Him. What did Jesus do? How did He respond? He stooped down and wrote in the sand as though He never heard them. Sometimes you have to ignore what the Devil is saying because he will try to back you into a corner. The Devil will say, "Here is what the Word says. Why are you looking and acting like this when here is what the Word says?" The Bible says, "By your words you are justified and by your words you are condemned. What saith thou? So what do you say about this, Jesus?" This is an effort to try and get you to say something. Some things are exposed in verse 6. "This they said, tempting him, that they might have to accuse him." But Jesus stooped down and wrote with His finger on the ground.

Using my imagination, I wonder what He wrote. I believe that as He was writing He began to reveal some things that caused the Pharisees to back up. I believe He wrote "some addresses" and "some names." Jesus knows all things. He knew where the scribes and the Pharisees were and decided to write some names. While we are writing someone else's name, Jesus is writing ours. Jesus knows where we work, what we do, and what our thoughts are. Jesus stooped down, but didn't bow. There are ways that you can stoop down without bowing first—Jesus didn't have to bow to get down. Jesus was very skillful in stooping down. In other words, I'm going to put myself up under Moses where God lives. He is literally saying, "If I get myself up under Moses, I will not come against what He said, but then I'll go down into the bowels of God, in Hell where I must be sin, and realize that I paid for what she did." He paid for that—Glory to God! Jesus stooped down.

Know this—we can't keep stooping down. At one point or another we have to really try to understand and ask ourselves, "Why am I like I am?" In being honest with God, we need to know why we do the things that we do. When you really the love the Lord you don't do things that make the heart of God bleed. When we do not totally surrender to God, He literally has tears streaming down His face.

Why do we do what we do? Jesus understood something about this woman that the scribes and the Pharisees weren't willing to understand. The Bible says in Exodus 20:5, *"Thou shalt not bow down thyself to them, nor serve them: for I the Lord thy God am a jealous God, visiting the iniquity of the fathers upon the children until the third and fourth generation of them that hate me..."* The sins of our fathers were upon us before we even set foot on the earth, and as a result this would affect several generations, but we can do something about this. Things took place before we got here, and the law was already set in place. It is Moses' law—the law of the Ten Commandments.

I'm so glad Jesus stooped down. There is such a thing as a generational curse. Something took place before we ever got here. I thank God for some of those who come from families where there were generations of preachers. Many in the body of Christ do not have that in their genes. There is something that exists that is called a "generational curse," where something is entrenched in us that drives us to do a particular thing because of our forefathers. This is one of the reasons you can have people who seem not to be able to get out of what this woman was in, and that is adultery. There are people who struggle with the demon of gambling. Some try to get away from alcohol but fall right back into it. Some cannot seem to get up out of lesbianism and homosexuality because it got entrenched in their genes a long time ago. How do we break this demon? God said, "The sin of the fathers came down on the children to the third and fourth generations of them that hate me." Don't forget where it all started! This woman was caught in adultery, in the very act, and I wholeheartedly believe that Jesus looked way past what she did, saw what her daddy and her mama did way back then, and said, "You just hold on, for very shortly, I'm going to die, I'm going to bleed, and I'm going to hell in order to get this thing off of you." Why did she do what she did? Just as it was with her it is with us—there are certain things in our lives that we will always be struggling or battling with, because of what our forefathers went through and failed to break. We must deal with this.

So many are crying out, feeling tormented because they want to get out and cannot. The apostle Paul said, "Who shall deliver me from this wretchedness that I am?" Paul ended up saying that he thanked God for Jesus, who would deliver him from this.

In Psalm 51 there is a shortcut. After David fell and messed up with Bathsheba, he asked God to have mercy upon him according to God's lovingkindness. David acknowledged that he messed up in his spirit. He realized that he had something against his spirit man. He cried out, *"According to thy lovingkindness, according unto the multitude of thy tender mercies blot out my transgressions. Wash me thoroughly from mine iniquity."*

What he is saying is this—I did the sin but not the iniquity. I had part in the iniquity, but that won't show up until later on. But the iniquity that I'm paying for, I didn't do. What is the iniquity? The iniquity is what your forefathers did. They did the sin, and it was transformed into an iniquity that was going to hunt you down. The iniquity follows you right down through the genes, and you don't understand why you struggle with gambling, homosexuality, lesbianism, drunkenness, and other sins.

David says in Psalms 51:3, *"For I acknowledge my*

transgressions: and my sin is ever before me." This particular sin, adultery and fornication, is always before him. David is being honest talking to God. Delilah broke Samson by being ever before him with the same question. Your children will do you that way. They are ever before you with the same question. In verses 4-5, *"Against thee, thee only, have I sinned, and done this evil in thy sight: that thou mightest be justified when thou speakest, and be clear when thou judgest. Behold, I was shapen in iniquity; and in sin did my mother conceive me."*

David was saying to God that the iniquity was on his mother before he was ever conceived and that it met him at the womb; that at the very moment of his conception he possessed a natural tendency and desire to commit adultery; and that he had nothing to do with his pursuing sinful desires and pleasures. I'm not saying that you can't do anything about it, because you can. What you're going through right now, the things that keep showing up and are ever before you, are what you have to deal with. If God has given you an assignment to do, you must continue until you complete that assignment, dealing with your challenges and the iniquities so you come through for God with a testimony.

In verse 5, David is saying that he was shaped in iniquity and in sin did his mother conceive him, and in verse 6, he is saying, thou desire truth in the inward parts. *"Behold, thou desirest truth in the inward parts: and in the hidden part thou shalt make me*

to know wisdom.'' Wisdom is what Jesus used in order to get the woman out of the rut that she was in. Many people have knowledge, but knowledge without wisdom is dangerous. Wisdom is the ability to use knowledge. Jesus could not let them condemn this woman because this woman was going to win a lot of people to Jesus, if he could get the woman saved by instructing her that she was not just committing adultery, but acting in response to an iniquity that was following her and messing her up inside.

David further says to God, "Don't cast me away from your presence." That is exactly what the scribes and the Pharisees wanted to do to the accused woman —cast her away. Jesus was not going to throw the woman away. David goes on to say, ***"Cast me not away from thy presence; and take not thy holy spirit from me. Restore unto me the joy of thy salvation; and uphold me with thy free spirit. Then will I teach transgressors thy ways; and sinners shall be converted unto thee."*** David is bargaining with God! David's plea is that if God would just spare him, he could one day become usable and an asset to the kingdom. Don't ever get caught not working on your issues. Failure to work on your issues will lead to destruction. God is not so put out with you that He is ready to throw you away. God has His hand on you, and you are usable for the kingdom. You may ask yourself, "How do I get rid of what is on me?" Do what God says in His Word—repent. Ask God to forgive you for the sins of your fathers and to create in you a new heart and renew a right spirit within you.

Only God can make us a new creation and restore us to true godliness. Why did the scripture not say, "Create in me a right spirit?" It is because there is absolutely nothing wrong with your spirit, except that it needs to be renewed. Have you ever had anyone to tell to you that you had a "bad spirit"? You are convinced that it is bad, and now your spirit has been damaged. You must now renew it. There is a renewing effect that God wants to do with your spirit man so that it will regain strength. Immediately go before God and lift your hands so that God can heal your heart and spirit.

Repeat these words now: "God, I repent right now in the name of Jesus for my forefathers and for my foremothers. We repent right now, in the name of Jesus for our ancestors in the past. Father, forgive them for the iniquity and for the sin they have carried and they have started. Forgive them, God; forgive them, God, in the name of Jesus. Father, forgive me, for I have participated in the sin and in the iniquity. Forgive me, God. Forgive me, in the name of Jesus. Now Father, break the power, break the yoke, break the effects, and break the maneuvers of that iniquity in the name of Jesus. I turn to you; I want to serve you, in the name of Jesus. I want to be usable for you in the name of Jesus. Now, God I receive it right now in Jesus' name. Amen."

Now shout about it, for God has set you free! Say, Father, in the name of Jesus, I declare freedom!

If we don't break the generational curses in our

day, our children will have to wrestle with them. What God revealed to me is that the worst thing our forefathers could have done was to wrestle with some of the things they wrestled with and not tell us. We must tell our children when they come of age. If you have children already, and you wrestled with generational curses, they will wrestle with them as well because the curses become a part of them when they break through the womb. Tell them about the promises in the Word and the struggles you have made. Let them know that God has delivered them. How many boys and girls do we see today going to prison because that's the trend of their mother, father, or grandparents? Saints, you have the power residing inside you that has been put there by the Lord Jesus Christ to totally annihilate every single thing that your forefathers have left you to deal with. What you are wrestling with now, your parents wrestled with as well. I say to you, "Walk into some of the promises of God and step into the generational blessings that belong to you."

The Choice is Yours

There is a flip side to the generational curse: the generational blessing. As we begin to get into the blessing, we cannot overlook the generational curse because we have to cancel out something before something new can come. If you come into the generational blessing without paralyzing the generational curse, the curse will eat up the blessing. Then you come to a point when you'll wonder, what in the world happened to my blessing? You'll be like Esau, who asked, "Is there yet a blessing left for me?" And you'll have to answer that with the word "no"; there is not another blessing left for you, because the curse keeps eating it up. We must deal with the generational curse and line ourselves up so there is nothing left to eat up the blessing. Unfortunately, sometimes we slip back where we come from, which allows the Devil to continue to eat up what God blessed you with.

Some of us may have made some headway because we made very tough decisions to set up the blessing plan of God. After God starts to pour in the blessings, the Enemy sees how well you're blessed and allows people, things, and habits to come back to crush out the blessing. You must protect the blessings that God has given you. People can sometimes lead you away from the blessings of God. Determine if this individual is a spiritual Pac-Man in your life. What do people who come into your life add? If they do not come with anything, tell them to get lost. They will show you love based on sharing the most valuable thing that they have. There are all kinds of things that seem to sidetrack us. We are totally lined up for the blessing, and we are walking right into the blessing. All of a sudden, before you move through the door, something on the left distracts you, something on the right distracts you, and when you look that way, you miss the door. These are some things that we really have to understand because we want to stay lined up with the blessing so we don't miss out on what God is getting ready to do.

And there was a famine in the land, beside the

first famine that was in the days of Abraham. And Isaac went unto Abimelech king of the Philistines unto Gerar. And the LORD appeared unto him, and said, go not down into Egypt. (Gen. 26:1-2)

You can determine if you are going into Egypt based on whether or not this thing engenders bondage. If it leads you into bondage, then it must be Egypt. We are not to go down into Egypt. What choice would you make, generational blessing or curse? The thing that is a curse feels so good, tastes so good, and is so much fun. I wonder who said that sin wasn't fun? They lied to you! You've been in sin all of your life and having fun doing it. Even the Bible says that sin is a pleasure for a season. Your choices that lead you into bondage, sin, and the curse will result in pain because it is so pleasurable to sin and it only lasts for a season.

Let's see if you can apply some pain to that decision that you are about to make. Make a decision not to go by the way of sin, because if you fall to sin, the pain is too great. Choosing to become involved with someone only to find out he or she later became involved with someone else is painful.

God is giving specific instructions not to go down to Egypt. He is not saying to avoid relationships, to be afraid of relationships, or to put up a wall so high that nobody can ever get to you. Even though I started out in Washington D.C., I received clear and specific instructions from God not to do church in Washington, D.C. Why? A prophet is not without honor but in his own home, town, and country, and among his own kin. And God said don't go there to do church; I want you to go to a land that I will show you. That land was called Waldorf, Maryland.

God told Abram, ***"Sojourn in this land, and I will be with thee, and will bless thee."*** You have to watch how you handle people whom God is with. Likewise, when God is with you, people have to watch how they handle you. It is necessary to understand this so that you can understand what God is doing. If you go where God has not sent you, He cannot be with you. God cannot work for you just anywhere. God has very specific instructions for you where He wants you to be. This is the reason we are concerned about people who join God Is In Control Church before they understand the church's assignment to spiritually grow the body of Christ and to train leaders. You cannot grow properly if you feed on food that is not designed to systematically bring you up from one level to the next level.

There are six blessings that God imparts because of our obedience to stay in the land where He told us to stay: God will be with thee; bless thee; give to thee; perform the oath which He swore unto Abraham; make thy seed to multiply; and in thy seed shall all nations of the earth be blessed. Sojourn in the land that I will show thee, and all six of these blessings will come and run you down.

Remember this: God promised to give them not only cities but countries. Don't give up on your faith. We're tapping into the real mind of God, and most of us are believing God too small. God wants to give you countries. He wants you to have the cities, but He's aiming at the country. You have to come to a point within your life that when you know God is with you, you will go after it. If you don't go after it, then the thing that opposes you will look like a giant and even a giant can come down.

God continues to say in verses 3-4, *"...for unto thee, and unto thy seed, I will give all these countries, and I will perform the oath which I sware unto Abraham thy father; and I will make thy seed to multiply as the stars of heaven, and will give unto thy seed all these countries; and in thy seed shall all the nations of the earth be blessed."* Let us go all the way back to when God made a promise to Abraham, Isaac, and Jacob that all the nations of the earth be blessed, until we get all the way down to your name, shall all the nations of the earth be blessed. In your children or in your seed shall all the nations of the earth be blessed based on the fact that you passed it on to them. Lay hands on your children and say **"I transfer the blessing onto you."**

Note: One of the reasons men get into sexual sins is because they have no one to validate them. The only thing they have to validate them is their male organ. They use it as a form of validation at home, with their friends, or maybe with someone on their job. It is usually a woman who provides them with validation. If that one person crushes them, then they need someone else to validate them.

The blessing has to be transferred. We need years upon years of people validating the man and the woman by telling them that they are somebody, how great they are, they are fearfully and wonderfully made in God, they are who God said they are, and they will not need anyone else validating them. Why? Because your daddy is transferring the blessing, validating you. They won't need anyone validating them because they had validation a long time ago. Most men have never really been validated.

God said He would make thy seed to multiply as the stars of heaven. Staying in line with God's blessing will enlarge your capacity to receive. God is tapping us into the blessing, but you're going to have to agree with Him. There are two reasons that God is tapping you into the blessing: one is that He wants you to be able to leave an inheritance for your children and your children's children. The other reason He wants you to tap into the blessing is so that you will not only be blessed, but be a blessing. Whenever we try to grab it all to ourselves, we turn are not in the will of God. If you're not blessed to be a blessing, then you are not in the will of God.

I should be able to walk up to anybody in the body of Christ and say, "Give me fifty dollars." You ought to be able to go in your pocket and say, "Here you go." Now, that's the will of God. Remember when Saul was going to the prophet to ask him where his father's lost donkeys were? In the Old Testament, they always approached the prophets with something. He said, "When we see the man of God, what shall we give the man of God?" In other words, they never would approach the prophet without a gift. Understand this— the whole idea is they did not have to figure out where they were going to get it. That is the way God wants us. We should not have to figure out where we are going to get it. I believe God is going to so increase us this way because we have operated under the generational curse long enough. It is now time to operate in the generational blessings. They are what God wants to get to us, but what it means is that we are going to have to fall out of agreement with the Devil. The Devil has already agreed that you're barely making it, that you'll never be anything, your mother wasn't anything, your father wasn't anything, and you won't be anything either. The Devil has already declared that, but now what we have to do is fall out of agreement with what he declared.

Now we have to declare a whole list of things for ourselves. Let me give you an example of the "power of command." Most of you at some time will start to get a little scratchy throat and declare, "I'm coming down with something." Have you ever noticed that once you declared that thing the symptoms move at a rapid rate? Some have even gone to the hospital, feeling fine until the doctor says, "I suspect that this is what you have." Understand this: Before we ever go to the hospital, they are still practicing medicine. Lawyers practice law. In other words, they haven't mastered it yet. And they are practicing on you. Now there is nothing wrong with doctors. I appreciate doctors, and they can be your best friends when you are believing God for healing.

Doctors will tell you what to believe for! If the doctor suspects that you have a particular illness—don't go and declare what he says! You will leave feeling worse than you did when you first came to the hospital. You must go off and declare what God says about healing. It's the power of command. So what are you commanding or demanding to happen in the earth? Remember, you're created in the image of God and in His likeness, which means that you have His ability. So, when He says, "Light be!" and light is, when you say, "Light be!" light comes on. So you have the same ability that God has, and it's not something that you really earned; it's something that God deposited in you. When you have a revelation of this, then you will literally come into your place of blessing.

And Jesus came and spake unto them, saying, all power is given unto me in heaven and in earth. (Matt. 28:18)

Every measure of power (exousia), meaning all God-given authority, has been given to me. The Devil doesn't have any authority. Anything the Devil does on the earth he does illegally. The only reason the Devil is able to do things and he never gets any repercussions from what he does is that we, the law enforcement agents, are not doing anything about it. When the Devil starts doing things in our lives and in the lives of the people around us, we are the ones that enforce the law, but we don't know what to enforce because we do not study the law, which is in the Bible. Because we don't study the Word, then we don't know when we are agreeing with the Devil.

And the seventy returned again with joy, saying, Lord, even the Devils are subject unto us through thy name. And he said unto them, I beheld Satan as lightning fall from heaven. Behold, I give unto you power to tread on serpents and scorpions, and over all of the power of the enemy: and nothing shall by any means hurt you. (Luke 10:17-19)

Some of the things that we desire are the very things that we are agreeing with the Devil on. God said that nothing by any means shall come on you and nothing shall hurt you. With that kind of understanding right there, you can go ahead and take the land. For whatever you desire, God will always place a desire in your heart. Because of the laws of the earth, God cannot just automatically give you this desire until it becomes your desire. God will not rush in to do it unless you ask Him. When you ask, then watch Him do it. Many of us go after things on our own, and God is not listening. How do you know if it is God that has dropped that desire in you? Ask yourself why you want it. If you are provoked because someone else asked, then it is covetousness and lust, and you're asking God to satisfy your lust, He won't do it. How will you know if it is a God-given desire? First, you will not be thinking about it, and second, you did not ask for it because of a selfish reason. When you don't know where it came from, you'll just believe it's time. When the desire is truly from God, you will move on to the next place and gain a mental picture of what you want inside yourself; you don't say anything to anyone about it; and when you declare it, it will manifest.

What do you do while waiting? The whole time you are fellowshipping and in prayer before God, gaining a mental picture. Do you realize this will work for your unsaved loved ones? You can change your life and somebody else's life. Do you want your loved one saved? Just gain a mental picture and see them saved. You're not thinking about what is present; you're thinking about what is in the future for them. See your family, yourself, your church, and your business in the future. Declare what you see in the future to come into you now. There are so many things that hold us in the past. You may have experienced having someone to literally speak things over your life, especially leaders, and now you are finding that there are particular things that hinder you. **Fix it and forget about it!**

Whenever we leave and cleave correctly, success is inevitable. There is no way to stop a person who leaves and cleaves correctly. If you did not leave correctly and didn't know any better, you can't go back. If you are presently in a marriage that is full of problems, and you finally come to realize that you married the wrong person, what do you do? **Just fix it!** There is no such thing as marrying the wrong person. Erase it from your mind. I would like to also warn the singles who were once married. Where you left off in the last marriage is where you will start when you remarry. You cannot shut down and think that you will escape the test. You will have to face the same test over and over again until you pass it. This is the reason why it is not wise for you to jump out of situations quickly. Some of your parents have never won in this area, and as a result the test was left for you. God is totally determined that someone is going to pass the test, so deal with it!

When someone declares that particular things are going to happen in your life, what is your position? Do you just accept and agree with what they say? Based on what they have said to you, do you tell yourself that you will never amount to anything? You may not consciously be thinking this, but it is showing up in your actions. You are preparing for what they said. What do you do? When the Enemy comes in, we should flood ourselves with the Word of God and take a bold stand against what they say is going to happen. People's words have released a demonic force against what God desires for us in our day. The Devil rides upon the authority of the believer. So we cannot even joke around with what has been said about us. Things that we say, even in a joking manner, will allow the Devil to ride on our authority. We have to understand that we must fix our minds to tap into the blessing; otherwise we're preparing to fail. **Anyone who is not preparing to win is already preparing to fail!**

Fill Your Mouth With the Word of God

Do not let anything or anybody stop you from receiving what God has for you. You must fill your mouth up with the Word of God. It doesn't matter what kind of curse tries to follow you or stop you from what God has for you. What is God saying about what He desires to bring you into? Some of us desire to have lots of money but have never read one book or listened to one tape. If you suddenly came into a lot of money, would you know how to manage it? Most of us would say "no." Why? Because we have never read one book on the subject.

Many of us say that we have been called into ministry and become upset when we don't get the opportunity. I ask you, "How many ministry classes have you taken to prepare yourself for what God has called you to?" Your niche is what will make you rich; so how many books are we reading and how many tapes are we listening to in order to get there? The things that are more important to us are the things that will dominate our thinking. There is a wealth of information out there that will move you towards what you want. How badly do you really want it? Whatever it is you desire to be successful at, go underwater for sixty seconds with that image in mind, and when you get to the point of gasping for breath, when you want what you say you want that badly, you'll come into it. Nothing will get in your way of accomplishing it. Sometimes we will declare what we want but are not willing to meet the obligation to get it. When you are ready to sacrifice everything, you'll come into it. You will pay the price, and God who sees all will respond to the fact that you are paying a price. You must have the mindset that you are going to win by filling your mouth with the Word of God. **Meditate on the Word both day and night!**

And the LORD said unto Joshua, This day have I rolled away the reproach of Egypt from off you. Wherefore the name of the place is called Gilgal unto this day. (Josh. 5:9)

God has some things that He wants you to come into, and He is determined to bring you into them, but He first wants you to know that the reproach is rolled away. God has rolled away the generational curse you've been carrying. Many of us are trying to work for that which God has already done. He is waiting on you to accept the fact that it's a done deal and the reproach has been permanently removed. You can now come into what He has for you! The reproach is something that you may have done that caused you to get a bad name or discredited your integrity. What is it that has held you up in your past? It's already been rolled away, but we're still laboring with it, trying to figure out what's going on.

When we understand what grace is and what God has done for us through and by Jesus Christ, we'll really understand what God is doing in our lives. He's tapping us into something that did not cost us a thing. In this grace dispensation, most denominational and traditional people have already impressed upon us that there are particular things we have to work for. God spoke to me, saying most people are still trying to work their way to heaven. He never casts a person into hell because the person sinned. People go to hell because of sins or rejection of Jesus Christ. Jesus paid the price for us to go to heaven, but this is not a license to sin. Some may be judged as a law keeper. The reason is for suggesting that the only way through is by the keeping of the law by works. James 2:10 (Amplified Bible) says, **"For whosoever keeps the Law [as a] whole but stumbles and offends in one [single instance] has become guilty of [breaking] all of it."** Do you want to operate under grace or works?

We must clearly understand that the only time we can condemn people to hell because of works is when we are free because we keep the whole law, not offending in one point. Let's focus on moving into the place that Jesus earned for us. The first thing we can do is to receive His Son, our Lord Jesus Christ. Some of you right now may not receive your fullest blessings on the earth because of living in sin. God won't bless us in our mess. We're not even talking about going to heaven, for that's almost a guarantee. How do we reach God's best on the earth? Say "no" to things that are off limits. If you want God's best, you cannot live the Devil's worst or it will clog up your blessings. Every time you sin you'll have to think, What am I getting ready to kill now? Every time you sin, something has to die; every time you make the right decision, you are causing something to prosper; and every time you make a godly decision, you are causing something to live and abound and receive God's best in abundance.

How to Proclaim Victory

Do you know what dancing does in the kingdom? When we are dancing, shouting, and giving God the glory, we are jumping on the Devil's head proclaiming victory in the name of Jesus. Every time we dance on the floor in the Devil's camp we proclaim victory in the name of Satan against God. Dancing is a spiritual thing, and the Devil did not come up with it. Miriam danced before the Lord after the victory at the Red Sea because God was getting the glory. When Saul was oppressed by demons, David played to provide him peace from the attack. Consider what you're dancing for before you dance your next dance. Don't you dare think that the Devil won't try you in what victory you feel or know that you received. The job of the Enemy is to attack your mind to hinder your process. Therefore I want to show you how to deal with the Devil and keep the control of your mind. The mind is where the battle will take place. Remember that the Devil can't take authority over you, neither can he make you do a thing. Therefore his strategy must be to get you to move and do the damage yourself. The trick of the Enemy is to affect your mind, which is totally conscious of the things that surround you. The greatest tools that Satan will ever use are the things that you are accustomed to. **There is a "battle" in the mind; will you win?**

Chapter 6

Winning the Battle of the Mind

Present Your Body A Living Sacrifice

I beseech you therefore, brethren, by the mercies of God, that ye present your bodies a living sacrifice, holy, acceptable unto God, which is your reasonable service. And be not conformed to this world; but be ye transformed by the renewing of your mind, that you may prove what is that good, and acceptable, and perfect, will of God. For I say, through the grace given unto me, to every man that is among you, not to think of himself more highly than he ought to think; but to think soberly, according as God has dealt to every man the measure of faith. For as we have many members in one body, and all members have not the same office: so we, being many, are one body in Christ, and everyone members one of another. Having then gifts differing according to the grace that is given to us, whether prophecy, let us prophecy according to the proportion of faith; or ministry, let us wait on our ministering: or he that teacheth, on teaching; or he that exhorteth, on exhortation: he that giveth, let him do it with simplicity; he that ruleth, with diligence; he that sheweth mercy, with cheerfulness. Let love be without dissimulation. Abhor that which is evil; cleave to that which is good. Be kindly affectioned one to another with brotherly love; in honor preferring one another; not slothful in business; fervent in spirit; serving the Lord; Rejoicing in hope; patient in tribulation; continuing instant in prayer; Distributing to the necessity of saints; given to hospitality. Bless them which persecute you: bless, and curse not. Rejoice with them that do rejoice, and weep with them that weep. Be of the same mind one towards another. Mind not high things, but condescend to men of low estate. Be not wise in your own conceits, Recompense to no man evil for evil. Provide things honest in the sight of all men. If it be possible, as much as lieth in you, live peaceably with all men. Dearly beloved, avenge not yourselves, but rather give place unto wrath: for it is written, Vengeance is mine; I will repay, saith the Lord. Therefore if thine enemy hunger, feed him; if he thirst, give him drink: for in so doing, thou shalt heap coals of fire on his head. Be not overcome of evil, but overcome evil with good. (Rom. 12:1-21)

We all fight with something in our minds. We won't master this as long as there is a Devil. We need to learn how to win the battle of our minds. One of the things to first understand is that there are a real battle and a real enemy. The Devil doesn't "fight fair," and he will hit you at your weakest area. He will never shoot at your strength. In the Book of Romans the apostle Paul has to deal with particular issues at the church of Rome. He knows the tremendous struggles that they have had and that some of the things that they would be dealing with would hit them right in their minds.

Apostle Paul is speaking to Christians about sanctification and that they should purify themselves from everything that contaminates the body. He is begging them to do this. When we think about our bodies, we're not just talking about what we just put in our stomachs; we're talking about everything across the board—what we look at, what we say, and what we do. We engage in activities that form pictures in our mind. If you spend all day viewing scary movies and that night before retiring for bed you begin to pray, the Devil will inevitably bring evil thoughts to your mind. He will have you envisioning demons coming out of the closet, and you will find yourself watching to see if they will actually come out. Perhaps you may have been watching all these nature movies and the Devil will begin to give you pictures of what you saw. The Devil will have you relive what you have allowed to come into your mind and distract you from praying to God. How does this happen? You didn't present your body as a living sacrifice!

There are times when I have to rebuke the Devil for a particular amount of my prayer time. Why? Because the Devil tries to invade my mind by sending thoughts about this and thoughts about that. If a thought comes, do not entertain it! Dismiss it! Only then will you be able to get a clear word from God. In other words, be not fashioned or shaped like another, or do not conform to the world's system or the world's way of doing things. We must realize that the present world system is under Satan's rule. Many of us conform to the world's way even in what we put on our body. Let's look at "to fashion or shape one like another." A lot of times what we do not understand is that the clothes that we wear are often fashioned after the world. Many of the fashion designers pattern their clothes according to a mental picture they get from the world. When we wear them, we are fashioning ourselves with the same spirit that they're operating in. We should particularly be careful when purchasing jewelry such as necklaces, rings, earrings, etc., and especially when dealing with Oriental and African art. Why? Because some may attract demonic influences. We have to get the background on what we are wearing, particularly of the emblems that we may place on our bodies. Wearing this type of jewelry or having it in your house will cause demonic activity or influence around you and could very well affect your mind. So don't be conformed to the world's way of doing things.

Let me share with you an experience that I had while working. There was a lady at my job who had these little knick-knacks called "trolls." The little dolls had wild hair, and many of the people who saw them thought that they were cute. The real idea behind it was that those were emblems of ancient gods that were actually leaning towards demonic worship. When we have things like that in our house, we wonder why there seems to be demonic influence—our children will start acting wild and having erratic behavior. It actually stems from what other people called gods in our houses, keeping those things around because we think they are cute. Whenever there is demonic activity around, it affects your mind. Strongholds will invade your mind. *"...but be ye <u>transformed</u> by the* *renewing of your mind..."* The word "transforms" means to change radically in inner character, condition, or nature. We are to turn our life and will over to God so that He can transform us into the godly person He wants us to be. Proverbs talks about "the heart of a child," that the heart of a child has been deceitfully wicked from its youth, but the rod of correction will drive it far from him.

When you look at that as the mind, you will understand that you didn't have to learn how to do wrong; you automatically knew how to do wrong. We had to learn how to do right. We didn't have to fashion our minds to think of wrong; they automatically thought of wrong. We had to renew our minds by meditating on the Word of God. Everything that we watch on television is programmed in our minds. Our minds are just like a computer.

Let me explain to you about the awesomeness of the mind. The Bible says that God brought to Adam every last creature for him to name. There is not a creature that God brought before Adam for which he duplicated the name. When you really think about it, there are over one million bugs and Adam, in the awesomeness of his mind, named them all and never duplicated a name. Likewise, he named every creature that walked upon the earth, not only the ones that crawled. When we think about renewing our minds, we'd have to understand that most of our brain is not being used. Your physical strength is determined by your mind. You will find people who will tap into drugs and become addicted. I remember some time ago while in the hospital waiting room, a very tiny young lady who was high on drugs became extremely upset when they did not wait on her fast enough. She actually picked up a nurse and threw her across the room. It took three policemen and four doctors to place handcuffs on her. She got completely psyched out on what she was on and it gave her strength that she didn't realize she had. Her mind was renewed from where it used to be to another level and provided physical strength in her body.

Are You Suffering From a Stronghold?

When your mind is suffering from a stronghold, it will not let your heart believe. The first thing you have to do is to sow the Word of God into your mind so that it will get down into your heart. When your mind and your heart agree, then you will be able to break the strongholds and receive manifestation. If we're going to renew our minds, we have to keep the Word of God in our mouths so that transformation can take place. If you don't keep the Word in your mouth, you will fizzle out on God! **Know this:** Even though you may have the Word of God in your mouth, the Devil will still try to get into your head! In fact, the demonic activity will increase! James 4:7 says, *"...Resist the devil and he will flee from you."* When we do not resist the Devil, we actually give him all the energy to bombard us with unhealthy thoughts. **Resist the thoughts that he sends!**

Gain Control of Your Mind

Unless we win the battle of the mind, we will all likewise be miserable. Some of us before today were miserable, because we weren't winning the battle of our minds. If we are going to have peace that surpasses all understanding, we will have to start a process in our lives of winning the battle that is in our minds. There is a real enemy that comes up against our minds, and we're going to have to start a process of winning that battle. Financial lack will cause a battle to wage war against your mind that will rip up every single thing in your life and make you totally uncomfortable about the things you really need to do. If you are not able to control something you care about, the Devil starts to lie to you in your mind. This happens to men when they find themselves in a position where they cannot take care of their homes. The Devil wages a war in their minds that will bring them down if they continuously listen to what he says. We find with women that if the home is not the way that a woman really wants it to be, then the Devil will wage a war in her mind to point where she does not want anyone to visit or to drop by. The Devil may be waging war against your mind in order to shut down your spirit. Out of your spirit comes life. If the Devil cannot directly get to your spirit, he attacks your mind so that your mind will shut your spirit down.

The Lord spoke something to me about the Jezebel and Delilah spirit as it relates to battling the mind. He said that Delilah is not dead and Jezebel remains alive. This has very little to do with a woman if it is in context with scripture. It is called a "her" because the male carries the seed, and the woman reproduces and multiplies the seed that was planted. Anytime Jezebel or Delilah is mentioned, it is as a "her," because anytime you give yourself over to Jezebel, it reproduces whether you are a man or a woman. In other words, if you yield yourself to it, it will reproduce bondage in your life.

If you yield money in bad places, it will reproduce financial lack for you. We need to make sure that we kill Jezebel and Delilah. They work hand in hand. Delilah finds out the secret to your abundance, your strength, or your walking in absolute victory in God. Then Jezebel comes along and kills it. When sin comes in and the Devil starts to bombard your head with things that bring bondage in your life, it's either a spiritual Jezebel or a spiritual Delilah that shows up in order to kill your anointing. God has gifted or anointed each one of us for a purpose. He has you going in a particular direction, and He wants you to come into the fullness of your destiny.

God put you on the earth to fulfill what is in His mind regarding you. The Devil bothers us in order to kill things that are in the mind of God. It's not about you. God needs us to yield to Him to fulfill what is in His mind. If we yield to the Devil, the Devil will kill what's in the mind of God. You must fulfill God's purpose because He has already spoken it. Sometimes we go through tremendous trials because God is trying to get something onto the earth, and we're rebelling against what God wants. He wants us to submit to the process so that we can fulfill the promise.

Do You Have Control Over Your Mind?

Before we fulfill God's promise, we must first win the battle of our minds. If every one of us were honest, we would confess that we have a war waging in our minds. The apostle Paul says when we want to do good, evil is always present. But if we look past what stands around us and look to God, who is our help, then what's standing around won't matter.

It's time now to get control over what your mind says to you and gain peace. If you don't control your mind, then chaos is inevitable. You mind will say that folks are talking about you when they hadn't thought about you; chaos will tell you something is wrong when there is nothing wrong. To gain control of your mind, know that God has touched your life so that you cannot be the same. Use God's Word as your point of reference and your measuring stick. Measure your life by the Word of God; don't measure it by brother so-and-so or sister so-and-so. "How I would love to be like Brother So-and-So." You don't know what he had to go through in order to be that. Focus on your own life. God says He keeps whatever you commit to Him. You commit it; He'll keep it. I committed this ministry and myself because I cannot even keep myself and need God's help. Commit your life and your mind to God, and God will give you peace that surpasses all understanding.

ABOUT THE AUTHOR

"Jeremiah 1:9-10 (KJV) 9 Then the LORD put forth his hand, and touched my mouth. And the LORD said unto me, Behold, I have put my words in thy mouth. 10 See, I have this day set thee over the nations and over the kingdoms, to root out, and to pull down, and to destroy, and to throw down, to build, and to plant."

Bishop Rodney S. Walker I is a dynamic prophetic voice whose ministry is renowned as being a catalytic agent for understanding and maturing in the prophetic.

A native of Washington, D.C., Bishop Walker is the Founder and Senior Pastor of Heritage Church International, established in 1990 in Waldorf Maryland. He serves as the General Overseer of Bishop R. S. Walker Ministries - formerly Another Touch of Glory Ministries - that covers national and international churches, para-church ministries and businesses.

He is spiritually covered by and accountable to Dr. Michael Freeman of Spirit of Faith Christian Center in Temple Hills, Maryland. He is also submitted to his Spiritual Father, Bishop Ralph L. Dennis of Kingdom Fellowship Covenant Ministries in Towson, Maryland.

In addition to being a graduate of the Jericho Christian Training College, Bishop R.S.Walker received his Doctor of Divinity Bishop R. S. Walker's training by versatile and equipped instructors, guidance from his Mentor, as well as submission to his Spiritual Father, has developed him into a well-balanced, grounded, and seasoned prophet.

In 1999, Bishop Walker founded the School of the Prophets. The School has locations in Waldorf and Baltimore, MD, Raleigh and Wilson, NC, Abuja, Nigeria, York, Pa, and has been hosted throughout the United States and beyond using online streaming.

In addition to equipping and training in the prophetic, Bishop Walker has also assembled a body of Prophetic Presbyters who assist him in managing the great assignment God has set to his hands.

Bishop Walker is the author and publisher of over 10 books including: The Prophetic Prayer Journal, Raising Prophets of Character, Becoming a Proven Prophetic Voice, The 21st Century Prophet, The Renaissance Prophet, and The Father/Son Encounter all of which prove to be phenomenal resources of the serious believer's library.

Among Bishop Walker's many accomplishments, is that of being a devoted husband to his lovely wife, Pastor Betty Walker, and a loving father to his eleven wonderful children.

Bishop Rodney S. Walker's ultimate goal is to fulfill

all that God has purposed for his life and to effectively lead those placed in his prophetic and pastoral care. His love for God is evident in his preaching, teaching and zeal for ministry. You will experience the wind of the Spirit through this Man of God.

Order Form

Bishop RS Walker Ministries
2760 Crain Highway
Waldorf, MD 20601
301- 843-9267 or 877-200-8967
Fax 240-585-7093
www.bishoprswalkerproducts.com
e-mail: admin@bishoprswalker.com

Name

Title
Date

Church/Ministry

Address

City   State
Zip

Daytime Phone   E-mail

Items Ordered:

Description	CD	DVD	Book	Qty	Total
Raising Prophets of Character Book $14.95					
School of the Prophets 15-week Course $190.00 Disc $110.00					
School of the Prophets Live Training $250.00					
School of Prophetic Intercession $200.00					
Prophetic Dominion Series $34.00 $47.00					
Renaissance Prophet's Manual $33.95					
The Art of Tongues Book $ 9.99					

Raising Prophets of Character Prayer Devotional $14.99

Creating Habits for a Functional Life $14.99

The Father Son Encounter $16.95

The Fundamentals of Faith (6-CDs) $50.00

Power of First Fruit Offerings (6-CDs) $30.00 $60.00

Shipping Information:
Add $5 for Priority Mail
for first item and
$1 per each additional item
MD add 6% sales tax

Method of Payment:
Please charge my: Discover   MasterCard   VISA   AMEX
Card Number: Expiration Date (Month/Year):

_____

_____

Signature (as shown on credit card):

Check or Money Order
(made payable to Bishop RS Walker Ministries)

For Speaking Engagements contact:
Office of the Bishop Administrative Staff
Phone: 301-843-9267
Fax: 240-585-7093

www.ingramcontent.com/pod-product-compliance
Lightning Source LLC
Chambersburg PA
CBHW072005060426

42446CB00042B/1833